The Principles of Social Policy

Also by Robert F. Drake

*Understanding Disability Policies**
Understanding Equal Opportunity Policies (with Ken Blakemore)

*Also published by Palgrave

The Principles of
Social Policy

Robert F. Drake

palgrave

© Robert F. Drake 2001

First published 2001 by
PALGRAVE
Houndmills, Basingstoke, Hampshire RG21 6XS and
175 Fifth Avenue, New York, N.Y. 10010
Companies and representatives throughout the world

PALGRAVE is the new global academic imprint of
St Martin's Press LLC Scholarly and Reference Division and
Palgrave Publishers Ltd (formerly Macmillan Press Ltd).

ISBN 0–333–76337–8 hardback
ISBN 0–333–76338–6 paperback

This book is printed on paper suitable for recycling and
made from fully managed and sustained forest sources.

A catalogue record for this book is available
from the British Library.

Library of Congress Cataloging-in-Publication Data

Drake, Robert F.
   The principles of social policy / Robert F. Drake.
      p. cm.
   Includes bibliographical references and index.
   ISBN 0-333-76337-8 – ISBN 0-333-76338-6 (pbk.)
      1. Social policy. 2. Social justice. I. Title.

HN16 .D75 2001
361.6′1–dc21   2001021232

10   9   8   7   6   5   4   3   2   1
10 09 08 07 06 05 04 03 02 01

Printed in China

To Gillian Drake

Contents

List of Figures

List of Tables

Acknowledgements

No book can be written without the help of others and I owe special thanks to my colleagues at the University of Wales, Swansea. Despite the unremitting pressures confronting them, Ken Blakemore, Anthea Symonds and Sam Clutton have given me unstinting support, boundless encouragement and most of their coffee. My thanks also go to a generous friend and mentor, Professor Maurice Broady, whose wisdom and advice I value greatly. Equally, I am indebted to Tim Stainton and Bruce Haddock for putting me on my mettle with their incisive and pellucid comments. I also want to acknowledge the contribution of some very fine social policy students, especially Fiona McDonald, who relished the chance to turn the tables and criticise early drafts of chapters.

At Swansea University we are fortunate to benefit from the superb knowledge, skill and dedication of our Library and Information staff. In particular, Lis Parcell and her team are of unequalled excellence. Within the School of Social Sciences and International Development I must mention Cindy, Julia, Kim, Jen, Liz, Sarah, Carol and Eryl. Whatever their actual job titles may be, miracle-working seems to form the larger part of their daily routine. After so much help I must confess that any errors are entirely my own fault.

Formal acknowledgements are due to those who granted me permission to use copyright material. I am grateful to the Office for National Statistics for allowing me to use the table in Chapter 6, and to Palgrave for permitting me to draw on material from Chapter 2 of my book *Understanding Disability Policies*. The material in Table 2.1 (taken from Reid, I., Williams, R. and Rayner, M. (1991) 'The Education of the Elite' in Walford, G., *Private Schooling, Tradition, Change and Diversity*) is reprinted by permission of Paul Chapman Publishing. Some data in Table 8.1 are from Burrows, R., Pleace, N. and Quilgars, D. (1997) *Homelessness and Social Policy*, reprinted with permission of Routledge. My thanks also go to the Department of the Environment for permission to use other data in Table 8.1. For her sagacious counsel I am again beholden to my editor at Palgrave, the incomparable Catherine Gray. Last, but not least, I pay tribute to my family: my parents and my wife Gillian, to whom this volume is dedicated.

ROBERT FRANCIS DRAKE

1

Introduction

Aims of the book

My main reason for writing this book is that in seeking to explain social policy the majority of existing volumes seem to adopt one of two approaches. They either provide a developmental or historical account of the welfare state, or they act as a sort of compendium in which one may find key ideas in education, housing, health, social security, social work and so on. It appeared to me that what was lacking was a text which explored the values and principles that stand behind social welfare. The elucidation of policy is not easy and on occasion we must inch our way blindly through the political smog. There is nothing new in the fact that sometimes governments and their opponents value the art of persuasion above the candid enunciation of truth. Down through the ages flimflam and 'spin' have found a ready niche in the political world. My aim here was to look beyond the everyday slanging match of party politics and give calmer scrutiny to the values and principles that underlie social policies in democratic states (Baldock *et al.*, 1999; Colebatch, 1998; Parsons, 1995; Bulmer *et al.*, 1989; Vincent, 1987; Hill and Bramley, 1986; George and Wilding, 1985). There are, then, three main goals: first, to investigate the values that guide state action; second, to understand the relationship between principle and policy; and, third, to suggest ways of analysing policy outcomes.

The state: values and purposes

There are of course many different views as to the 'proper' roles a state should play and the specific responsibilities it might assume towards its citizens. At one end of the spectrum it may be strongly

1

held that few obligations exist and that the state has little business to interfere in people's everyday lives. From this point of view the state has only very limited scope (if any) to reallocate or redistribute scarce resources from one group to another (Green, 1990; Seldon, 1981; Friedman and Friedman, 1980; Joseph and Sumption, 1979; Nozick, 1974; Hayek, 1960). There are, however, other standpoints where it is contended that the state has a central duty to ensure the well-being of its citizens and a responsibility to guarantee them the basic constituents of a civilised life, even if such a guarantee carries with it the need for regulation of certain social activities and some redistribution of social goods such as wealth, property, status and opportunity (Commission on Social Justice, 1994; Marshall, 1992; Andrews and Jacobs, 1990; Plant, 1990, 1988, 1984; Drabble, 1988; Novak, 1988; Lister, 1990). Clearly few, if any, contemporary Western governments occupy ground at the very extremes, of anarchic free-for-all on the one side, or totalitarian control over every aspect of economy and society on the other. Instead, they seek to balance the need for collective social welfare against respect for individual freedoms. Similarly, they try to lay down some desiderata for the allocation of social goods without putting their market economies at risk (Clasen, 1999; Midgley, 1997; Hill, 1996; Esping-Anderson, 1990).

It is clear that political decisions about the extent and purposes of government intervention can have profound implications for the contours of citizenship. Where a government holds that the role of the state is minimal (perhaps limited to seeing fair play in the way that interactions between individuals happen), its focus will be on regulating *processes* as opposed to securing particular *outcomes*. In these circumstances, a government may have no truck with the redistribution of wealth and will also look with little favour in the direction of expansive social policy. It is unlikely, for example, that there would be, under this sort of administration, any thoroughgoing social security system to protect the poor from destitution. Instead, there might only be laws to prevent fraudulent contracts (or other kinds of criminal exchange) between people (Friedman and Friedman, 1980; Nozick, 1974).

However, where a government's values and beliefs – and subsequently its policies – are concerned with outcomes as well as processes, it may intervene in pursuit of particular goals. For example, a government might wish to limit the extent of social inequalities in a society or secure fresh opportunities for some disadvantaged groups (Jordan, 1998; Mandelson, 1997; Marshall *et al.*, 1996;

Labour Party, 1994; Atkinson, 1983; Bevan, 1952). Social security may be introduced to relieve poverty, housing policies created to prevent homelessness, education policies designed to alleviate ignorance, and health policies enacted to combat disease. Perhaps the key issues here are about how societies (and their governments) decide what is fair and appropriate, how they determine what obligations states should fulfil towards their citizens and what protections they should afford them. How do states define 'social problems', and how do they formulate their responses towards them? On what principles, therefore, may social policies be based? These questions stand at the heart of this book.

Principles and social policies

Social policies are not randomly created. They are guided by (albeit sometimes rather opaque) values, principles and objectives. The task here is to review some of the key principles found in contemporary politics and I deal, in the chapters that follow, with concepts such as freedom, equality, justice, rights, diversity and citizenship. The reader will see that for each of these principles we must ask not one question, but two. First, by what principles (if any) do political parties claim that their policies are guided? Second, how do governments conceptualise the principles to which they claim allegiance? Because concepts like justice and freedom are open to many kinds of interpretation this latter question is crucial. On occasion a professed adherence to principle may be mere rhetoric; however, governments do draw up policies to embody the values they espouse and so we need to know how such values are conceived and understood. The matter is essentially one of definition.

It is also important to recognise that policies can articulate values of a very different order than those to which I have referred so far. We· may find that a government chooses to promote, not equality, but privilege. Equally, it may create advantages for people of a certain clan, caste or colour. Legislation could advance the interests of some nominated social group or class, or give endorsement to some cult, sect or religion. Accordingly, policies may be designed to achieve aims not directly connected with any substantive policy area at all. Health policies may be devised to cure the sick but also to set the interests of one racial group over another. Or, again, housing policies could be used less to eliminate homelessness than to segregate members of one race or community from members of another. Education policies might be intended to favour one social class to the detriment of another. These kinds of policy are based on a belief now alien to (and rejected by) most, but not all, Western political parties, that some kinds of people are intrinsically different to other kinds and thus warrant different treatment. Indeed, it is a view that has underpinned social phenomena such as neo-Nazism, racism and apartheid, and is most often found in parties and groups on the extreme right of politics (Thurlow, 1999; Bulmer and Solomos, 1999; Gregor, 1997; Eatwell, 1995; Beinart and DuBow, 1995; Laqueur, 1991; Miles, 1988; Meredith, 1988).

Because values and beliefs can have significant impacts on policy outcomes, it is important that we should be able dispassionately to analyse the principles that stand behind any particular set of policies. Accordingly, the third main theme of the book is policy analysis.

Policy analysis

To document the quantitative effects of government actions is, on its own, little more than a descriptive activity. We may agree that the comparison of actual outcomes against initial intentions is important, but as policy analysts we must also discover and understand the values and principles from which policy intentions were developed. Policy analysis is difficult on two counts. First, on a practical level, there's many a slip 'twixt cup and lip. Between the formulation of aims and the achieving of results, there are countless internal and external pressures at work that may thwart the successful achievement of a government's original aims (Blakemore, 1998). As a result, it is not always right to assume that actual outcomes are indicative of original intentions (Parsons, 1995).

Second, policy principles may be neither harmonious nor mutually reinforcing (Hill, 1993). To begin with, aims such as securing citizenship, promoting equality, preserving the freedom of the individual, furthering justice and pursuing equality of opportunity are open to question. Exactly what do these concepts mean? Moreover, do the principles which underpin modern social policy coalesce in any rational way, or are they liable to be contradictory? For instance, there may be occasions when, in order to secure the liberty of the community, it is necessary to constrain, prevent or outlaw certain deeds and actions. The matter becomes one of balance. Can policies confer freedoms on some without infringing the rights of others? Is freedom of the individual reconcilable with other potential policy effects such as the redistribution of wealth? These several questions (of process and of principle) make it difficult to analyse policy, but they do not render it impossible. Definitions can be elucidated and conflicts of principle made visible (Hill and Bramley, 1986; Apthorpe, 1979; Rich, 1979; Rossi and Williams, 1972). Ultimately, policies derive from values. While it is true that every reader has his or her own set of values and will therefore favour or reject particular policies accordingly, we can at least be clear about what values and principles are in play, and why, exactly, any particular set of policies receives our approbation or opprobrium.

The structure of the book

Values, principles and purposes

In Chapter 2, I explore the transmutation of values and principles into policies which in their turn produce more tangible outcomes. There is a distinction to be drawn between those principles focused on substantive areas of policy, and other, more general principles overarching the entire range of a government's manifesto. I will argue that these 'meta principles' are derived from, and thus support, prevailing norms, values and beliefs.

How a society defines concepts such as 'justice', 'freedom' and 'equality' will directly affect the contours of the policies it creates. For example, some values will foster plural policies, able to accommodate diversity and difference within a population; they will treat the norms and beliefs of different groups and communities with equal recognition and respect. However, other values and principles may reject diversity and instead attempt to impose uniformity by promoting just one set of values to prevail over, and so displace, others. It follows that the values and principles which stand dominant in any society will have a profound effect on the direction and purpose of policy.

Liberty and equality

My aim in Chapter 3 is to explore the meanings of two ideas often cited as overarching policy principles: *liberty* (or *freedom*) and *equality*. Scholars have attempted many different ways of defining both of these terms and have sought to understand how the two concepts affect each other. Some writers (Scruton, 1982; Joseph and Sumption, 1979) have treated freedom and equality almost as if they were mutually exclusive, arguing that freedom is predicated on inequality – how can *choice* be meaningful if there are no variations or differences? These scholars conclude that absolute equality precludes freedom and expunges liberty. But others (Crick, 1992; Plant, 1990, 1984; Thomson, 1969) have come to the view that one special sort of equality is vital to society: equality between people in the extent and scope of liberty available to them. Some writers refer to this 'equality of liberty' by another name: 'equality of opportunity'.

In analysing particular social policies, it is important that we understand the specific meanings that are ascribed to 'freedom' and 'equality'. We need to discover whether policies are intended to expand or curtail certain freedoms, widen or reduce an existing degree of inequality. Most governments have sought to reach a compromise between the ambit of individual freedom and a desire for some measure of communal equality. While some have favoured individual autonomy come what may, others have been concerned to limit the gross disparities in fortune that unfettered markets can bring. And yet both have claimed to subscribe to the mediating principles of justice and equality of opportunity.

In contemporary Western thought, few libertarians and egalitarians adopt extreme definitions of 'equality' or 'freedom'. Perhaps communist regimes in China and Albania came closest to any real attempt to impose sameness through ideology, education, dress, work, leisure and other aspects of everyday life (Lawrence, 1998; Winnifrith, 1992; Kropotkin, 1987; Schnytzer, 1982; Stefanaq, 1981; Karol, 1967; Schumann, 1966). But if equality (in the sense of sameness) has few adherents, the potential evil of absolute freedom is also easily demonstrated. Persons who are under no social constraints, and under no threat of retribution, may with impunity visit acts of great cruelty and violence on others powerless to defend themselves. Totalitarian regimes of the right (Nazism, Fascism) have, perhaps, most readily turned to their own ends this Nietzschean sense of unfettered 'freedom' (Hollingdale, 1999; Owen, 1995).

In practice, of course, those who cherish freedom do not think of the word in this malign sense. When writers such as Hayek (1960), Scruton (1982) and Minford (1991) write about freedom, they are seeking to fend off arguments by socialist commentators that it is legitimate for a state to redistribute wealth from rich to poor. Each of these 'pro-liberty' writers predicates the autonomy of the individual – at least in part – on the economic operation of a free market. 'Liberty' in this sense is shorthand for arguments against state interference. For these authors, the crucial role of government is to protect individuals from incursions either by fellow citizens or by the state itself. Their accounts are important not only for their theoretical contributions to what we understand by freedom, but also because they inspired much New Right social policy in the 1980s.

However, critics of New Right thinking (for example, Jordan, 1998; Marshall *et al.*, 1996; Labour Party, 1994; Marshall, 1992; Lister, 1990; Plant, 1988) point out that there are occasions when 'freedoms' exercised by some can entail constraints for, and even repression of, others. The question, then, is one of boundaries. At what point should 'freedom' cease to be legitimate, when do inequalities amount to harm? John Stuart Mill recognised this problem and offered one possible solution when he argued that civil liberty meant that 'no one should be prevented from doing anything *unless it harmed his fellow citizens*' (Jaeger, 1943: 9).

Our specific interest in the meanings of 'liberty' and 'equality' is their relationship to social policies. Government policies may restrict the scope of individuals or enhance it, may reduce the inequalities between people or exacerbate them. As policy analysts we would want to know, therefore, what definition of 'freedom' and what conceptualisation of 'equality' are being employed by a government when it formulates a particular policy, and what impacts the subsequent outcomes have for the freedom of individuals and the disparities between them.

Before leaving Chapter 3, one other key concept is considered: equity or fairness. I have said that many governments claim to pursue a 'fair' balance between individual autonomy and social equality. But what does 'fair' mean in this context? I have already mooted one conceptualisation: equality of liberty. One key approach to establishing 'fairness' in recent years has been a search for equality of opportunity.

Equality of opportunity

In the second main part of Chapter 3, I explore the notion of 'fair inequalities' and discuss the concept of equality of opportunity (Blakemore and Drake, 1996; Kandola *et al.*, 1995; Drabble, 1988;

Plant, 1984). In brief, egalitarians argue against inequalities only where they arise *unfairly*. There may be differences (or, if you will, inequalities) between people, but are these disparities necessarily unfair or undesirable? There are many strands of egalitarian thinking but most might agree that inequalities are only unfair where there exists a distribution of opportunities which unjustly favours some section of the population over the rest (Brown, 1988; Baker, 1987; Frankel, 1983; McCloskey, 1966). A main concern of policy analysts is to discover how particular policies affect the distribution of opportunities within a population. Are certain groups privileged over others for certain purposes? If so, on what grounds? What kinds of opportunities are expanded, what kinds are closed off? Here we face not only the practical difficulty of tracing distributions of opportunities and their impacts, but the even greater problem of determining the fairness or otherwise of any particular distribution of opportunities. What is meant by 'fairness' or 'justice'?

Concepts of justice

It would be an extraordinary government that declared as its aim the promulgation of unjust policies. But what are we to understand when governments claim that their policies are just? The purpose of Chapter 4 is, first, to explore meanings and definitions of justice and, second, to clarify what kinds of inequalities, if any, may be 'just'. This is a critical question given the importance of these values in the political landscape of contemporary Western democracies.

Some definitions of justice are focused on the *processes* of exchange between human beings. Nozick (1974), for example, argues that it is sufficient for justice to be served that the transactions between individuals be conducted fairly, irrespective of any consequences that may flow from such transactions. Other writers, however, deal not only with processes of interaction, but also with *outcomes*. Here I draw particularly on the thinking of John Rawls (Freeman, 1999) to explore the proximity between justice as fairness and equality of opportunity. For Rawls (1972), justice is concerned as much with results as with processes. In his theory of justice, Rawls enunciates two fundamental principles. First (drawing on Mill [1859]), justice prevails where each person has an equal right to the most extensive basic liberty compatible with a similar liberty for others; and second, social and economic inequalities are so arranged that (a) they can reasonably be expected to be to everyone's advantage and (b) any privileges that result from inequalities are attached to offices or positions open to all.

Rawls's second principle demonstrates how inequalities may not only be fair, but may provide greatest benefit to the least advantaged. Furthermore, in arguing that positions (offices) should be open so that all may aspire to them, and that each candidate should undergo the same fair tests of fitness, Rawls is describing equality of opportunity, not equality of results.

Finally, I discuss some more recent work by – amongst others – Kymlicka (1990), Walzer (1983), Young (1990) and Phillips (1998, 1992, 1987), all of whom, in differing ways, represent 'justice' not as some extrinsic metaphysical entity susceptible to formulaic definition, but as a social artifact, a variable property of specific spheres of activity within each particular society and, as such, much harder to pin down. For Walzer, there are – potentially, at least – as many definitions of justice as there are separate spheres of life in diverse and unique cultures. Here, any particular notion of justice is a product of agreed distributive criteria for the social goods in each sphere of life at any given time. The root questions, then, are: What particular conceptualisation of justice does a government employ when it formulates its social policies? What aims does it believe to be fair, and why?

In deciding what is just and unjust, lawful and unlawful, societies and governments are also defining and setting out the *rights* of citizens (with respect to the state and with respect to each other). However, the definition of rights is not a straightforward matter. Some writers (for example, see Jones, 1994; Freeden, 1991; Dworkin, 1977) contend that not all rights are contingent on state definitions of justice and law. They describe a further class – human rights – that exist above and beyond the immediate disposition of any particular state at a given time. These human rights may be traduced, but not extinguished. The next chapter therefore explores the influence of rights and needs in the creation of social policy.

Rights and needs

Chapter 5 explores the notion of 'rights'. There are many definitions of what constitutes a 'right' and in order to analyse social policies it is important to know what kind of conceptualisation a government is using in any specified context.

Clearly, a government's view as to what constitutes a 'right' will depend on its understanding of justice. Where a state intervenes to secure social justice (in the terms set out by Marshall, 1992) it will acknowledge rights concerned with equality of opportunity and access to certain necessities for civilised life. However, where a state is concerned less with outcomes than with the processes of interaction, it will acknowledge rights akin to contractual obligations, but may be more reluctant to establish or acquiesce in rights pertaining to outcomes (including, perhaps, welfare rights). It may be an over-simplification of his position, but we may think here of Nozick's (1974) argument that outcomes, no matter how undesirable, are not unjust as long as they are arrived at through voluntary and fair transactions between individuals. For Nozick, only fraudulent transactions are unjust.

But there is a problem here. Are 'rights' independent of our definitions of justice or are they subordinate to them? As I indicated earlier, some writers (Jones, 1994) argue that there are certain rights (human rights) to which we are entitled irrespective of local definitions of justice. It is argued that this special class of rights stands superior to those created locally. Moreover, human rights are regarded as imprescriptible and inalienable. They are, therefore, not susceptible to alterations in law and practice (Jones, 1994).

Where rights are infringed, two consequences follow: the harming of citizenship and the failure to meet 'need'. For Doyal and Gough (1990), the consequence of a need, so created, is an obligation on society, through the medium of the state, to compensate the individual by rectifying injustice (as defined within that society). Accordingly, the greater the 'distance' between the actual state of affairs and the restoration of justice, the more serious the need and more significant the right involved.

It is important to recognise that the rights acknowledged within a particular society and, just as importantly, those excluded, will be closely tied to conceptualisations of justice. A policy analyst will be interested in what kinds of right and need are acknowledged within social policies and what kinds are denied or ignored.

Finally in Chapter 5, I discuss 'empowerment' as a means both of meeting needs and of satisfying rights. Through resulting legislation social policies may confer rights or reject them. Equally, policies may either create needs or satisfy them. Beresford and Croft (1993, 1984) contend that where there are groups in the population whose rights are denied, means of empowerment are critical to their reclamation.

For the process of empowerment to take place, two things are necessary: first (and perhaps more simply), there may need to be some specific and tangible alteration in policy. But second, and more complex, the difficulty may stem not so much from the configuration of policy as from the structures of political power. Here the change would need to take place not only in the policy montage but also in the structure of government (and possibly in the structure of society itself) (Fraser, 1989; George and Wilding, 1984).

Problems concerning individual freedom, social equality, equality of opportunity, rights and needs are made all the more difficult to resolve when we recognise that governments produce policies in the context of plural societies. What may be a fair policy for one group may be unjust with respect to another. Some authors (Miller and Walzer, 1995; Phillips, 1991; Young, 1990; Williams, 1989) argue that sensitivity is needed in the levels and structures of policy creation in order to respond appropriately to the variegated circumstances that prevail in plural societies. Pluralism entails respect for diversity and the acknowledgement of difference, and it is with these concepts that Chapter 6 deals.

Diversity and difference

Hitherto I have treated governments and societies as if they were monolithic and undifferentiated entities. In reality, however, this is not so and the words 'diversity' and 'difference' highlight the fact that modern communities are plural and ever-changing. Diversity refers not only to differences of culture and ethnicity, but also to differences in gender and sexual orientation, to physiological and cognitive differences between people, to differences in political values and beliefs (Hallett, 1996; Burrows and Loader, 1994). The key question for this chapter is what kind of vision of society does a government hold? Does it believe that fair treatment demands policies sufficiently complex to respond to different people in different ways in order to achieve fairness overall? Or does a government's world-view mean that the beliefs of one particular section of a population (for example white Anglo-Saxon Protestant males) are taken as the 'norms' to which others must aspire or comply?

Evidently, discriminatory consequences can arise when the values of one group prevail over those of others. In these circumstances, where policies favour a dominant sector of society, outcomes differ for individuals according to the groups to which they belong and the values to which they subscribe. However, other kinds of policy may attempt to accommodate differences within plural societies and diverse cultures. Counter-hegemonic analyses by writers such as Abberley (1996; 1987), Lister (1997), Phillips (1991), Young (1990) and Kandola *et al.* (1995) all provide ideas as to what 'diversity politics' may look like. Their common theme is the liberation of subordinate social groups through the realignment of power relations with dominant groups or classes (Lukes, 1974; Gramsci, 1971).

Clearly crucial to this chapter is what we (and what governments) mean by diversity and difference. Accordingly, I begin with an attempt to define these terms as they are used today. The main bulk of the chapter is given over to an assessment of the impact that these concepts may have on the creation of policy. Where policies are guided by plural principles, they will be formulated in such a way as to recognise and acknowledge differences between people arising from such factors as their culture, race, gender and age (Miller and Walzer, 1995; Phillips, 1991; Young, 1990; Kymlicka, 1989; Williams, 1989; Fraser, 1989).The interplay of such differences will allow for the development of sensitive and diversified (as opposed to uniform) types of practice. At the same time, however, flexibility will be used neither as a cloak for discrimination nor as a basis on which to vary the quality of response and the treatment of citizens (Kandola *et al.*, 1995; Kandola and Fullerton, 1984; Behrens and Auluck, 1993). For example, recognising that the mobility of some (disabled) people depends on wheels rather than feet, equality of opportunity is maintained by principles and policies which produce flexible transport configurations rather than uniform (foot-based) designs (Drake, 1999; Imrie and Wells, 1993; Barnes, 1991).

However, where principles promote policies which sustain only the interests of a governing or dominant group, it is likely that 'nondominant' (the contemporary term is 'excluded') citizens will encounter disadvantages (Levitas, 1998; Roche and Van Berkel, 1997; Leigh-Doyle, 1996). For example, if a powerful group has a particular skin colour, a specific gender and economic potency, the application of their own values in the creation of principles *may* give rise to policies which create or enhance racism, propagate gender stereotyping, or produce an economic and social underclass (Brown, 1990). We may even go so far as to claim that in a plural society principles which do not accommodate diverse values and cultures are, of their essence, discriminatory.

Discrimination is a word that has attracted negative overtones, but it is possible to discriminate in a just way or in an unjust way. What matters is the basis of the differential treatment. For instance, in providing a service one may discriminate between people according to the severity of their need for that service, or one may discriminate using a criterion of no intrinsic relevance to either the service or the need. A policy which can adapt to, and respect, a variety of cultural values is one thing but a policy which varies its responses so as to denigrate or oppress some people whilst privileging other sections of the population is another.

I have said, then, that policy principles may promote the values of a governing group, but in doing so may lead to unjust discrimination against less powerful sections of the population. Ironically, however, these same principles may also have qualities necessary for the functioning of any society. By retarding change and encouraging some degree of uniformity they may support stability within whatever structures obtain. The direction of change will depend on the principles that prevail. While some will favour a more plural and diverse society, others could lead to a more restricted and uniform one.

Why should we be concerned about the impacts of principle and policy on different sections of society at all? Why does it matter if some are dominant and others are either subordinate or completely excluded? In Chapter 7 I deal with these questions through an examination of the concept of citizenship.

Citizenship

Early in the book it becomes clear that there are profound differences between writers as to the meaning of 'justice'. There is, however, considerable agreement that for justice – in whatever clothes – to prevail, each individual must enjoy the same status or quality of citizenship as every other member of that same society. Walzer (1983: 31, 32), a major proponent of localised and relativistic definitions of justice, agrees that 'the primary good we distribute to one another is membership in some human community' and 'statelessness is a condition of infinite danger'. For Walzer (1983: 312–6) justice is relative to social meanings, but social meanings are produced by social actors. Exclusion from such processes leads to oppression. Each person must be able to participate in agreeing the rules of the society in which he or she lives. (I say *be able to participate* because some may choose not to contribute to these processes.) If some are forcibly excluded they are not citizens, but slaves (Walzer, 1983).

For societies and governments who understand justice only as fair processes and contracts, there can be enormous inequalities between citizens, but all still have the same rights of citizenship to protect them against fraudulent transactions. For governments that extend the meaning of justice to cover outcomes (i.e. the patterns of distribution of social goods) citizenship will imply certain social rights and set limits on the extent of allowable inequality.

What is citizenship? From what I have said so far, it is clear that the answer to this question varies according to culture, community, time and place. In Chapter 7 I explore different definitions of citizenship and distinguish between autocratic and democratic understandings of the term. So, for example, where a society is governed by an elite, it is possible that different individuals will experience different qualities of citizenship according to their proximity to that elite. Some may even be excluded from citizenship altogether. In other, more egalitarian societies, the quality of citizenship may be more uniform and more generally shared. The extent to which principles have positive or adverse effects on society will depend on the values on which they are based and the definition of citizenship they underpin (Turner, 1993; Barbalet, 1993; Andrews, 1991).

Citizenship in autocratic societies. In a hierarchical and autocratic society, policies will be shaped by the values and principles to which a governing group subscribes, and citizens will be measured against, and treated according to, dominant norms. People will be judged in the light of criteria determined by those who hold power. At the extreme this may lead to injustice through *differential citizenship*, in which equal consideration is *not* extended to all people, but some are treated preferentially above others. Practical examples of these kinds of criteria may include differential treatment based on skin colour, religious status (e.g. caste), age and gender (MacKinnon and Gatens, 1998; Smith, 1996; Ali, 1991).

Citizenship in plural societies. Some communities subscribe to principles that accommodate competing values. Such societies are likely to favour social policies that treat people not identically, but equitably, irrespective of their colour, creed, age or gender (Barbalet, 1993; Andrews, 1991). In Chapter 7 I consider the key implications of citizenship in plural societies. Briefly and first, policies will not force people to conform to some partial dogma or doctrine. Second, any inequalities between citizens will arise from their different sociocultural locations rather than their politico-economic circumstances. Third, plural principles encourage – indeed, demand – the participation of people in their own governance. Fourth, because such principles encourage the devolution of power, social change is intrinsic to them. Fifth, plural principles are also, by definition inimical to totalitarian or centralised forms of government. *Policies formulated using plural principles are, in fact, created by those whom they affect.*

Plural principles thus envisage a very active conceptualisation of citizenship. The chapter recognises, however, that some thorny problems remain. First, what degree of fragmentation (how many value systems and cultures) can plural principles accommodate without resulting in anarchy and chaos? Second, inequalities however they arise may still privilege some, and those who gain advantageous positions could then use their greater influence and power to challenge the plural principles on which protection of sustained diversity depends. It follows that plural principles must also be inflexible in one unique sense: they cannot bestow different values (or powers) of citizenship. Equally, we must acknowledge that just because plural principles allow different value systems and cultures to coexist, this does not guarantee that each of these value systems will of itself be free of autocratic features. Some value systems may therefore threaten plurality and, with it, the quality of citizenship enjoyed by some individuals.

The final section of the chapter anticipates the next part of the book which is concerned with policy analysis. Ultimately, policy is to be understood in terms of its consequences for individuals, the scope of their liberties, the fairness with which they are treated by the state and by others, the acknowledgement of rights and meeting of needs. In short, policy must be judged according to the quality of citizenship that it yields, and each of these elements is crucial to any comprehensive analysis of social policies.

Policy analysis

Definitions of concepts like equality, justice, liberty, rights and difference are essentially contested. In Chapter 8 I argue that the contours of 'real-life' social policy are determined first, by the locally active definitions of these principles, but second, by the external influences of an uncertain world. For a preliminary but crucial question, then, how far are social policies really the products of principle, and to what extent are they merely reactions to ongoing events? Do social policies accord with the values, beliefs and intentions of their instigators, or do they arise from more immediate responses to the more immanent pressures of the everyday world?

While acknowledging the disruptive impacts of unplanned and unexpected social events, and while recognising the thick fog of party politics, I nevertheless contend that detailed and meticulous scrutiny of policy contexts, aims and outcomes can reveal much about the values and intentions that have guided their creation. By the end of the book the reader should be able to discover the motivating forces and principles underpinning any particular set of social policies, and should be able to measure these against the outcomes that flow from them.

Changing political contexts

The final task, set out in Chapter 9, is to relate the theoretical ideas discussed in the main body of the book with the development of policy and practice in the real world. In determining the extent to which policies are principled or reactive, we must assess the context in which they have been created. In recent years two major trends have been discernible. First, nation states (and particularly national economies) have become increasingly susceptible to the vagaries of global economics and supranational political structures (Giddens, 1999). Second, within Western democracies, political power has been devolved, at least to some extent, to internal regions. We may think, for example, of the increasing local autonomy enjoyed by the Basques in Spain, the Walloons in Belgium and the separate republics that once constituted the USSR. Similarly in Britain, certain powers have been devolved to a Scottish Parliament, a Welsh Assembly, and a complex power sharing administration in Northern Ireland (Bogdanor,1999; McCrudden, 1998; Mackintosh, 1968).

The final chapter concludes with some emerging questions about the future of social policy in a fast-moving world. If social insurance was a child of the nation state and a response to mass industry, the contemporary era of political and economic restructuring may hold serious implications for welfare. A once unified and unionised workforce is undergoing profound change as a result of new, fragmented and compartmentalised patterns of work. Moreover, the autonomy of the nation state is being attenuated by global economic forces and by local and cultural pressures for the devolution of power (Midgley, 1997; Ledger and McCracken, 1995; Wolf, 1992; Downing and Bazargan, 1991). The auguries suggest that the welfare states of the old century face an uncertain future in the new one.

In summary, the key aims of this book are to recognise the multi dimensional nature of the values and principles that stand behind political thought, to acknowledge their importance in shaping the contours of social policy, and to recognise the centrality of their influence over real outcomes in the everyday world. In the next chapter I consider the concept of a 'policy principle' before moving on, thereafter, to scrutinise in more detail the individual principles that I have now introduced.

2

Principles of Social Policy

Introduction

This chapter is about the connections between values, principles and social policies. It explores the place of values within political ideologies and assesses the influence of principle over policy. We see the importance of values and principles when, beyond their immediate concrete objectives, politicians refer to some broader, and perhaps less tangible, desiderata. So, for example, the British prime minister, Tony Blair, has written:

> I have always believed that politics is first and foremost about ideas. Without a powerful commitment to goals and values, governments are rudderless and ineffective, however large their majorities (Blair, 1998: 1).

> We are in politics to pursue certain values... Since the collapse of communism the ethical basis of socialism is the only one that has stood the test of time. This socialism is based on the moral assertion that individuals are interdependent, that they owe duties to one another as well as themselves, that the good society backs up the efforts of individuals within it... only by recognising their interdependence will individuals flourish, because the good of each does depend on the good of all (Blair, 1995: 12).

The importance of moral values is echoed in the writing of a previous Labour chancellor of the exchequer, Denis Healey:

> I am a socialist who believes that the Labour Party offers the best hope for Britain's future... I do not believe that I or my colleagues are perfect; nor have I ever believed in the perfectibility of man. But my faith in the moral values which socialism represents... remains undiminished (Healey, 1989: xiii).

This theme of moral imperative was summoned directly by Harold Wilson in his sense of political purpose:

> The Labour Party is a moral crusade or it is nothing (Harold Wilson, quoted in Owen, 1991: 89).

The aim of improving social conditions has stretched across party political boundaries in Britain. A previous Conservative prime minister, John Major, said that he was:

> attracted to the Conservative Party because ... it cared for the weak, the poor and the old, but unlike the Labour Party it did not demand a lifetime of adherence to a class struggle. It saw people as individuals, not as political troops. [Conservatism] argued for the opportunity to build security and ownership and wealth (Major, 1999: xvii).

In his book, *The Middle Way*, another Conservative, Harold Macmillan, declared:

> The meaning of social progress is the liberation of men from want and the unfolding of new possibilities of a more satisfactory and abundant life. A political policy is, or ought to be, one thing consistent in itself and in its application to the whole field of social effort (Macmillan, 1938: 4).

But for other (New Right) Conservatives, the overriding principle has been to minimise government rather than use it as an instrument of social justice. Margaret Thatcher argued that governments were:

> 'blind forces' blundering about in the dark, and obstructing the operations of markets rather than improving them ... I was again asking the Conservative Party to put its faith in freedom and free markets, limited government and a strong national defence (Thatcher, 1993: 11, 15).

We see, then, that down the years leading politicians have declared that broad beliefs and values guided their policy and practice and, as Harold Macmillan argued, governments seek to apply their principles not just to one area of policy, but to an entire programme. What we notice, however, is that perhaps every government (and opposition party), almost as a sort of mantra, claims adherence to a very similar set of values. The emphasis may vary. Where some stress 'freedom', others emphasise 'equality', but most argue that there exists a reciprocity between the state and the individual in which freedoms are counterbalanced with social responsibilities, and communal equality with respect for individual privacy and autonomy (Crick,

1984). Nevertheless, close analysis of policy detail can reveal stark differences in what different governments mean when they use words like justice, fairness and liberty. Freedom for whom? Freedom to do what? Freedom from what? Some laws may protect people so that they are free from oppression or exploitation, other laws (or the absence of law) may supply so much liberty (through lack of regulation and constraint) that some people are left free to exploit or oppress others (Moorehead, 1989; Torrance, 1977; Jenkins, 1970). As scholars, our task is to discover how the authors of policy understand these terms; as citizens our aim is to judge their desirability.

The chapter begins with a preliminary discussion about the role of values and principles in the political sphere. My interest lies in the ways in which values and principles stand behind, and inform, more tangible social policy, its aims and outcomes. The second part of the chapter distinguishes between different kinds of policy purposes. I contrast specific (constitutive, substantive or intrinsic) policy purposes with more overarching, general, or 'meta' purposes. These latter may include the desire to achieve greater equality, to secure liberty, to honour rights or to empower disadvantaged groups. Clearly, these kinds of aims can apply to any or all areas of social policy. In later chapters I try to show that though these words are often used together, they are actually very different types of concepts. Some (*equality*, *liberty*, *justice*) may be broad or concomitant objectives for policy whilst others (*empowerment* or the *fulfilment or denial of needs or rights*) may be the result of policy. What they all have in common is that governments may cite them as generic policy aims above and beyond specific intentions in particular areas of activity.

The third part of the chapter concentrates on the purposes of policy. These may include, for example, to effect change or maintain the status quo, to promote specific norms or accommodate diverse values, to differentiate between people or treat them the same. Other purposes may be more specific: for example, to create or remove institutions or to allow or prohibit certain practices or activities (Colebatch, 1998; Parsons, 1995). The final part of the chapter is about the scope and influence of principles over policy. Here I argue that the configuration of policy and practice at any particular time and place will depend, at least in part, on the principles which stand dominant in the society in question. These principles will, in turn, depend on the values and beliefs to which any government and society subscribes. We begin with the question: What are values?

Values and principles

Traditionally, scholars have attempted to define values in many ways. So for example, Mukerjee (1964) distinguishes between simple preferences ('I value my privacy and enjoy solitary occupations') and moral imperatives or 'oughts' ('Thou shalt not kill'). Unfortunately, determining the status of values is not a straightforward matter, for as Graham (1961: 13) tells us:

> All propositions are meaningless unless they are either tautologies (such as 'Two and two make four') or are verifiable by sense experience. Since moral and aesthetic pronouncements belong to neither class they are neither true nor false, but meaningless. 'Honesty is a virtue' and 'You ought not to steal' are expressions of approving and disapproving emotions, like 'Hurrah!' and 'Alas!' There can be no fruitful dispute over questions of value except in terms of tastes and goals which the disputants happen to share.

For Graham, then, values are somewhat amorphous concepts, they do no more than embody certain preferences and goals. However, Griffin (1996), whilst accepting their heterogeneity, argues that values are neither necessarily capricious nor short-lived objects. Griffin points to their historical quality: values are handed down from generation to generation and exhibit both durability and tenacity. Griffin argues that this persistence is not drawn from any natural stability in the expression of preferences or tastes; instead such degree of permanency as there may be springs from a different source: that of *utility*. The values most likely to persist are those that prove useful either in sustaining life, in preventing pain, or in promoting happiness. However, because people may stand in circumstances different one from another, they may espouse different values. It is common, therefore, to discover contradictions between different sets of values whether they be voiced as preferences or as ethics (Boucher and Kelly, 1994; Moore, 1959; Russell, 1949).

The *Oxford English Dictionary* defines a principle as 'an origin or source of action' and as 'a fundamental source from which something proceeds, a primary element, force or law which produces or determines particular results'. In a further definition the *OED* declares a principle to be 'a general statement or tenet forming the ground of, or held to be essential to, a system of thought or belief. A fundamental assumption forming the basis of a chain of reasoning'. In the present context, I use the word principle to embody the values and beliefs to which a group or government subscribes. A principle thus transposes a general set of values into tenets guiding the formulation of doctrine and of policy.

Political ideology: clusters of values

What kinds of principles have philosophers and politicians placed at the heart of the doctrines they espouse? History has given us a number of distinct schools of thought including anarchist, fascist, liberal, social democratic, socialist and communist. What separates these doctrines is their view of society, their beliefs about the proper role of the state, and particularly the extent to which (and indeed, the ways in which) a state may intervene in the lives of its citizens. At one extreme, it may be thought that there should be no authority beyond the individual. Here, each person commands absolutely the conduct of his or her own life and bows to no other individual or corporate authority. So, for example, Rousseau (1762) argued that true liberty was to be found only in obedience to *self-imposed* law and a social contract was a matter of voluntary agreement between free individuals. The state is, in this sense, subservient to the individual. At the opposite end of the spectrum, a state may treat (at least some) individuals as chattels, allowing them to be bought and sold as the property of other people, or even making them slaves of the state itself. Hornblower and Spawforth (1998) provide the example of classical Athens in which there were publicly-owned slaves (*dēmosioi*) who might be put to a number of tasks, perhaps the worst of which involved labour in the state-owned silver mines of Laurium, where, the authors tell us, an early death amounted to a happy release. Here, then, the individual slave was entirely subservient to the state.

Other values and beliefs about the relationship between the state and the individual occupy territory somewhere between these two extremes. We may consider briefly a number of systems of political thought: liberalism; neo-conservatism; conservatism; socialism; communism, communitarianism and, finally, fascism. In what follows I explain briefly the basis of each of these political philosophies and make some initial suggestions as to the kinds of values each may promote.

Liberalism

Vincent (1992: 29) describes liberalism as a complex notion shaped by 'certain schools of thought'. He argues that classical liberalism comprises:

> a blend of ideas and strategies about how to acquire or defend liberty ... [it was] pledged to uphold liberty and the equal right of all individuals to equal freedom. Conventionally this freedom was understood negatively, namely, as freedom from arbitrary coercion.

Scruton (1982: 268) concurs, describing liberalism as 'a loose term used to mean a body of modern political doctrine ... that will guarantee the individual's rights against the invasions of the sovereign power'. Accordingly, he describes a liberal state as one in which the individual has strong objections to, and substantial rights against, the interference of the state. Those who believe in liberalism will thus seek to curtail the range and magnitude of government intervention. So Margaret Thatcher declared:

> What we need now is a far greater degree of personal responsibility and decision, far more independence from the government and a comparative reduction in the role of government. These beliefs have important implications for policy (Thatcher, 1968: 9).

Clearly, then, within a liberal state the individual is paramount and the scope for state intervention in the form of social policy is likely to be much constrained. The principle of equality, in this kind of regime, is likely to be constrained to equality of *potential* scope for freedom. That is, the extent or degree of liberty available to each individual will, in theory, be the same. However, the subsequent emergence of inequalities may, in practice, allow some a greater range of choices than others.

Neo-conservatism and conservatism

Liberal doctrines which promote the autonomy of the individual have been strongly represented by conservative political groupings. At their simplest, we may identify two main strands of conservatism: 'hard right' or neo-conservatism; and moderate or (in Britain) 'one nation' conservatism. The key differences between the two strands are of degree rather than quality. Neo-conservatives put their faith in the free market and desire to minimise state intervention through welfare programmes. Privatisation of state assets is a major plank of neo-conservative policy. Moderate or 'one nation' conservatism shares an impetus towards the individual and the market and away from state provision and control. However, this stance is mitigated by a sense of *noblesse oblige*, the idea that those who do well in life have a duty of care towards those who have been less fortunate (Raison, 1990). Accordingly, within moderate conservatism, the state has *some* role in securing the welfare of the needy, though without hindering the operation of commerce in a free market.

Socialism

For socialists, the collective features as largely as the individual, and the state has a far more significant role to play. Just as liberalism is to be understood in a multifaceted way, Vincent (1992) contends that there is a variety of 'socialisms'. These may be catalogued perhaps by type (scientific, ethical, Utopian) or by strategy (revolutionary, reformist). If there is a core idea, it is that human beings are not asocial. In the words of John Donne: 'No man is an island, entire of itself'. People are cooperative beings and as such community values are to be preferred over individualism.

Crick (1984) argues that three values stand at the heart of socialism. These are liberty, equality and fraternity. Crick is careful to draw a distinction between liberal and socialist understandings of liberty. He argues (p. 14) that a socialist view of liberty is not merely negative (of individuals being left alone, left in peace by the state) but also carries positive connotations of freedom to engage in society, to participate and help choose and fashion social futures. In tackling the meaning of equality as it is used by socialists, Crick rejects the notion that equality means 'sameness' and instead speaks of equality of treatment, consideration and opportunity. As to fraternity, Crick (p. 22) describes this value as 'an attitude of mind' in favour of tolerance, cooperation, mutual help, engaging together in common tasks and the generation of friendship. We may, perhaps, describe all these elements as the affirmation of the social, as well as the individual, world.

So, for example, socialism may entail, at least in some degree, the administration of a community's wealth on behalf of all. In particular, some things (such as the means of production) may be held in common ownership rather than possessed by any single individual or subgroup of the population. Where these circumstances hold true, social policies may be of enormous importance in the state's mechanisms for distributing material, economic, social and other resources.

Social democracy

Sullivan (1994) describes social democracy (in the British context) as a model of evolutionary (as opposed to revolutionary) socialism. He argues that social democracy as practised by the British Labour Party stemmed from two key influences, the incremental and expert administrative approach towards collective aims as advocated by the Fabian Movement, and the strong brand of ethical socialism which imbued the Labour Party with a moral and religious sense of obligation in the face of appalling poverty and squalid social conditions in the early twentieth century (Fraser, 1984; Thane, 1982; Tawney, 1926). Charles (2000) offers a broader functional analysis of social democracy linked less to the political history of a particular party and more to the process of class alliances, class representation, and their impacts on industrial development in capitalist states.

Communism

If social democracy represents an evolutionary form of socialism, then communism consists in a revolutionary form of socialism. For Scruton (1982), communism represents a more stringent and regulated strand of collective politics than does socialism. It follows that in such regimes, liberalism, in the sense of individual autonomy, is minimised. A community's assets are held in common ownership rather than in (an unequal distribution of) private property. Scruton notes that socialism was thought to be merely a stage on the path towards communism but the recent collapse of 'communist' regimes in Eastern Europe has cast profound doubt on the viability of communism as a workable doctrine. Speaking theoretically, within ideal communist states social and welfare policy would either not exist at all (since there would be no residual or disadvantaged groups in the population, all having equal access to the food, shelter, services and other materials they needed) or social and welfare policies and practices would comprise the normal distribution mechanisms of those basic goods (George and Manning, 1980).

Between these twin ideological clusters that have come to be simplified as liberalism and socialism (or collectivism), there stand a myriad of possible political arrangements incorporating strands from both families of thought. In the social democratic states that typify Western Europe, for example, one may expect to find a variety of attempts to balance the demands of the individual with the requirements of the community at large. Here, social policies will cover some, but by no means all, areas of needs and wants. Typically in such states, one may see policies concerned with the communal or state provision of services such as education, health, social security, some form of subvention for housing, and other environmental and emergency services (Cochrane and Clarke, 1993). The purposes, principles and policies developed in any society at any particular time will depend on the political values at play. Often, but not always, it will be possible to locate these values within particular political ideologies.

Fascism

Fascism is a difficult ideology to pin down. It is often spoken of as a phenomenon of the past. O'Sullivan (1983) asks whether fascism was an ideology at all, or merely a 'cult of action' without any doctrinal commitment. Sternhell (1994) argued that although fascism was a political force, it was born out of the desperate economic depression and chaotic social and cultural forces of the inter-war years: it was a revolt against rational or 'enlightenment' thought. Carsten (1976) contends that, historically, such mass support as fascism enjoyed came neither from the social elite, nor from the working classes, but from the lower middle classes. Kedward's (1969) analysis saw fascism as a synthesis of anti-liberal ideas, both rational and irrational. These included strands of nationalism, socialism, the cult of the heroic leader based on the philosophy of Nietzsche, and an evaluative categorising of people.

Though fascism may have been a historical phenomenon tied to a particular set of social, political and economic circumstances, it is important in the present context, first, because of the rise of neo-fascism, for example in Austria, and, second, because of the growth of particular fascist policies such as 'ethnic cleansing' in Kosovo and some of the Baltic states.

In terms of policy principles, fascist doctrines are based on the differentiation of human beings. In the twentieth century, under fascist dictatorships in Germany, Italy and Spain, distinctions were drawn between individuals on the basis of their religion, ethnicity, race and/or colour, their mode of living and their bodily state of being (Thurlow, 1999; Kedward, 1969). Even the most fundamental human rights (including the right to live) were denied people because they might be Jewish, or Slavic, or they were Romany gypsies, or they had cognitive impairments (Lifton, 1986). Under fascism, words like freedom, equality or fairness, if used at all, could only apply *within* social categories after people had been differentiated and segregated according to the classifications imposed upon them. The privileged groups might expect to be treated equally well, the oppressed groups dealt with equally badly. Democratic states revile fascism, but they also acknowledge that diluted strands of neo-fascist policy exist in their own societies through, for example, institutional racism, sex discrimination and prejudice against disabled people (Ferguson *et al.*, 1991).

Communitarianism

So far I have discussed doctrines in terms of relationships between the state and the individual as if these were two independent and bi-polar concepts. Kymlicka (1990) has argued that communitarians criticise the traditional pattern of left/right, collective/individual liberal politics. First, the very notion of 'independent' individuals must be questioned. Communitarians reject the liberal or atomised view of the self and subscribe to a theory of the social construction both of the self and of social reality: individuals are never independent of society (Frazer and Lacey, 1993). Communitarians argue that liberal political theory is wrong in conceiving of the 'person' as someone who exists autonomously and, in particular, independently of the social context which gives life its meaning and value (Mulhall and Swift, 1992). There can be no concept of an 'individual' divorced from the culture, values and practices of a community (Sandel, 1982).

Second, communitarians argue that a number of important issues are left out of traditional politics. Whilst government and economy stand at the centre of traditional structures of political beliefs, less attention is given to gender roles, the private versus public spheres of life, and roles within the domestic as opposed to the industrial and commercial spheres. Accordingly, Kymlicka (1990: 2) points out that communitarians believe that the evaluation of political institutions:

> cannot be a matter of judging them against some independent, ahistorical standard ... political judgement is a matter of interpreting the traditions and practices we already find ourselves in.

For Kymlicka the notion of socially constructed individuality means that there is a 'historical and communal "embeddedness"' not dealt with in traditional left/right political debate. This sense of the interdependence of the individual and the community is important when we come to discuss plurality – diversity and difference – within society in a later chapter. It is also important when we scrutinise 'universal' principles such as justice and equality.

Communitarians, then, are opposed to the idea of the 'neutral state' supported by liberal and neo-conservative thought. A neutral (i.e. non-interventionist) state allows individuals to operate unregulated in a free market. But communitarians aim for what Kymlicka (pp. 206–7) calls 'a politics of the common good' which comprises:

> a substantive conception of the good life ... a communitarian state is therefore a perfectionist state since it involves a public ranking of the value of different ways of life.

Kymlicka recognises that, at face value, these arguments appear both prescriptive and totalitarian. They seem to offer a conception of politics similar to that found in hard left doctrines such as Marxism. Kymlicka (p. 207) argues that appearances are deceptive:

> Whereas Marxist perfectionism ranks ways of life according to a trans-historical account of the human good, communitarianism ranks them according to their conformity to existing practices.

There is insufficient room here to pursue these arguments in greater depth, but the reader will find a detailed analysis in chapter 6 of Kymlicka (1990). What we need to ask is what kinds of social policies might communitarian-minded governments produce? Since the argument is that values would depend on social context, time and place, it is actually very difficult to say (see Chapter 6 below).

However, Cahill (1999: 482–3) argues that a key focus would be on quality of life:

> Communitarianism offers one response which stresses that communities need to be supported in enforcing their collective majority view about what passes for acceptable behaviour. Green [ecological] citizenship is related to this in the sense that, like communitarians, its exponents believe that individuals gain much of their identity from the local community and ... [communitarians] are active in fostering a social ecology of sound local relationships.

In summary, we may see how different sets of values underpin differing political doctrines. It therefore follows that the prevalence of a particular orthodoxy will have a critical impact on policy principles and purposes. It is to a consideration of these aims and objectives that I now turn.

Policy purposes

I have suggested that political ideologies comprise clusters of values. Within any particular ideology one may expect to find that values will usually have some affinity with each other. They will also inform the principles on which a government's policies are built. It is important, therefore, to be clear about the general or overarching purposes which policies may be intended to satisfy. I suggest there are five opposed pairs of generalised objectives:

- to keep things as they are *or* to effect change;
- to privilege a specific group *or* to treat all people equitably;
- to promote equality *or* to extend inequality;
- to promote a set of specific values *or* to accommodate diverse values;
- to change individuals (or groups) *or* to change environments.

Stability or change?

Principles may be developed in order to bring about certain changes or, instead, may be intended to resist change and uphold the way things are. Principles and policies designed for stability will support the prevailing norms, values and beliefs. In doing so, these prevailing

principles and policies will tend to exclude or subordinate any competing sets of values and norms (Plant *et al.*, 1980; Blackstone,
1973). Whether one believes that the maintenance of stability is good
or bad will depend on what it is that is being preserved. For example,
a society may be open, pluralistic, flexible, supportive of equal
opportunities, tolerant of various cultural and religious beliefs and
respectful of individual liberties and rights whatever a person's
colour or creed.

Equally, principles and policies may be designed to preserve the
pre-eminence of a single, narrowly-defined group within a population through maintaining discriminatory policies which afford privileges to some whilst disadvantaging others. In this instance, the aim
of stability would serve the interests of particular, powerful groups
and would affirm their values and beliefs to the detriment of other
citizens. Plainly, change may occur in either direction. Consider, for
example, the introduction into a hierarchical society of a principle of
equality or, alternatively, the advent of supremacist principles into an
open society.

Privilege or equal treatment?

Policy principles may either seek or resist change. But beyond this
they may also influence the way a government acts towards the population at large. Principles may foster the equal treatment of all citizens, or may reserve privileges for some to the detriment of others.
As a rather stark example of the latter, we may recall the era of
apartheid in South Africa. At that time policies across the entire spectrum of government were constructed on the basis of racial differentiation, and in particular were built on the assertion of white
superiority. Consequently in politics black people and those of mixed
race were disenfranchised (Meli, 1988). In education the apportionment of resources heavily favoured those schools attended by white
children (Gqubule, 1992) and in terms of access to health services
priority was reserved for white people (Seedat, 1984). The principle
of racial discrimination is 'particularistic' in the sense that it supports
the idea that one group of people should be treated differently from
another group on a single criterion (in this example, 'race' or more
particularly, skin colour). Moreover, this criterion is not intrinsically
relevant to the areas of policy affected. Crucially, the principle of
racial differentiation fails to be 'plural' in that it can accommodate no

other value system (for example, those of racial equality or, more broadly, equality of opportunity). Indeed, in this example the principle of white superiority was intended specifically to oppose and, indeed, exclude these competing principles.

Though I have just used a historical example from South Africa, there are other principles, active in contemporary British social policy, which lend support to policies that privilege particular groups or individuals. One value that has played a significant role in the creation of British social policies is economic incentive or differentiation. In primary and secondary education, for example, there is a public (free of charge) and a private (fee paying) sector between which (in theory) parents may choose. Indeed, choice stands at the heart of both New Labour and Conservative Party thinking. So, for example, a leading figure in Mrs Thatcher's cabinets, Norman Tebbit (1986: 3), has asserted that parents should be free to choose their children's schools, but other Conservatives, such as Lord Beloff (1984: 10), have acknowledged that 'the demand for private education is even now a function of the level of disposable income, and as with health, if a large private input were possible, the total expenditure might well be more considerable'. In other words, the vast majority of children who currently receive the privilege of a private education do so because their parents can afford the fees whereas some other children who might have benefited from a private education are unable to do so because their parents either could not or would not find the money needed. Equality of opportunity does not, therefore, prevail in this instance. The basis of selection (parents' access to sufficient wealth) is extrinsic to educational criteria. Governments have attempted to mitigate (or, more cynically perhaps, to obscure) unequal access by helping some children to gain a private sector education through mechanisms such as assisted places schemes. There are now, therefore, four groups of children:

1. those whose parents can afford to pay and are educated privately – whether they can benefit intellectually from that education or not;
2. those who are educated privately, having been successful in the competition for assisted places;
3. those who could benefit but who didn't get one of the limited number of assisted places, and whose parents can't afford to pay; and
4. the remainder (the vast majority of children), educated within the state sector and paid for through general taxation.

The argument frequently put in support of private provision is that the citizen is free to choose how to spend his or her money. Indeed, Kenneth Baker has gone so far as to argue that private schools constitute 'a key component of a free society' (Walford, 1990). A person may buy cigarettes and beer, or may invest in a son's or a daughter's education. There is, however, an assumption underpinning this argument that citizens command sufficient funds to be able to make such a choice. By giving up cigarettes, beer and the like, enough money would be saved to be able to send a son or a daughter to a private school. This assumption, that the same options are available to all, is only true where incomes and resources do permit choice, where, for example, the parents' income is sufficient to exercise the choice in question. Patently however, even if they were to devote the entirety of their incomes and capital resources, very many people in Britain would still command insufficient wealth to choose the more expensive options.

On its internet web site in 1998/9, the famous public school Charterhouse quoted £4,900 per term as its fee for students boarding at the school. The annual sum thus amounts to £14,700. Though that amount is higher than most private schools, it is by no means unusual in the general range of charges for private education. The independent advisers, Quest Financial Services, confirm that 'typically, in the UK, day school fees range from £650–£2,000 per term and boarders £1,500–£3,000 per term. Invariably the cost of this rises by more than inflation. For instance, in 1991 inflation was 4%, but school fees inflated by twice that at 8%. Basically, the cost of school fees is likely to double over the next ten years' (Quest Financial Services, 1999).

If fees for private education amount typically to somewhere between £5,000 and £15,000 per annum, how does this compare with net incomes in the UK? Table 15.2 of the *Annual Abstract of Statistics* (Office for National Statistics, 1998a) provides the necessary data. Of 25,800,000 working individuals, only 3,345,000 or 13 per cent have take home pay in excess of £20,000 per year. Evidently, access to private education is heavily restricted. Even if we leave out of the calculation all those who have no job at all, some 87 per cent of the working population cannot afford to provide their children with a private education. Other official statistics reveal that in 1996/7 just 595,200 from a total of 9,667,000 children were being educated privately, representing just 6.1 per cent of all pupils (Office for National Statistics, 1998b). Though some financial assistance may be available for poorer students, Tapper (1997) has shown that only

18 per cent of private school pupils receive any financial help, and for the vast majority such aid is very minor. It is most unusual for even half the total fees to be offset by an exhibition, scholarship or bursary. But does any of this matter?

Some hold that in any event education in the private sector is not necessarily 'better' than the public sector, it is merely different. However, data concerning students' higher education and eventual career outcomes effectively refute this argument. Walford (1990) established that in 1987 some 46.4 per cent of private school pupils left school with three or more passes at 'A' level. In the state sector, only 7.4 per cent of pupils achieved the same level of success. Unsurprisingly perhaps, Reid (1986) recorded that in 1984 52 per cent of entrants to Oxford and Cambridge came from the independent school sector. Moreover, Reid *et al.* (1991) have shown that although their dominance may have declined slightly over the past twenty years, it remains true that pupils educated privately preponderate in the top jobs (Table 2.1).

There are two key points here. First, prevailing values and principles may yield policies which either ensure equality of opportunity or instead buttress (or at any rate, leave undisturbed) existing privileges. We should note that policies can be as important for what they fail to do as much as for what they achieve. In this example, educational privilege leading to career advantage is protected under the clarion call 'freedom of choice'. As we have seen, the freedom referred to is by no means a universal one. My second (more general) point is that policies may be derived from constitutive or substantive principles (for example, devoting educational resources so that the differing talents and potential of each student may flourish), or policies may be subservient to some external factor such as the wealth of the parents of prospective or aspiring students. In this way principles may either secure privilege or guarantee equal treatment.

Much the same analysis can be applied to other areas of British (and more generally, Western) social policy. In the field of health, for example, private healthcare operates, like private education, according to the same extrinsic principle of economic differentiation. Those with the means to join a private scheme may expect to receive prompt healthcare whether or not there are citizens who, on medical grounds, need the particular resources more urgently. Again an 'external' principle is at play here; it is a principle sanctioned by government, one which determines access time to medical resources, and its essence is financial rather than medical. Those with insufficient funds may

Table 2.1   Pupils from independent schools: prevalence in elite
occupations

Career	Private or independent schools (%)	State sector and other (%)
Ambassadors (Heads of embassies and legations)	83.8	16.2
Judiciary (High court and appeals judges)	86.0	14.0
Bishops (Assistant bishops and above, C. of E.)	65.7	34.3
Bankers (Directors of clearing banks)	71.4	28.6
Civil Servants (Under-secretary and above)	53.2	46.8
Army (Major general and above)	76.3	23.7

Source: adapted from Reid *et al.* (1991: 21, table 2.2)

receive identical medical treatment in the end, but typically have to wait much longer to receive it. For example, in June 1998 the total number of people in England waiting to go into hospital for treatment under the National Health Service was 1,287,500. Of these, 30 per cent had been waiting for more than six months, and 5.6 per cent had been waiting for more than a year (Government Statistical Service, 1999). Similarly, at the end of September 1998 some 437,000 people had been waiting more than three months from the date of referral for an outpatient appointment (NHS Executive, 1998).

To recap, policies may protect or promote privilege on the one hand, or they may support equal treatment on the other. The actuality will owe much to the values active in the creation of policy. Some principles will produce policy that is comfortable with inequality, others will not.

Equality versus inequality

We may see, then, that principles may lead to policies intended to differentiate between groups in the population, having the effect (intended or unintended) of privileging some whilst penalising others. Perhaps the general point to be made here is that principles may inform policies which in their actualisation either reduce or enhance differences between people. Within a state whose values promote individual autonomy as opposed to group collectivity, principles and policies will not attempt to ensure equal outcomes. Instead, individuals will be encouraged to make their own way in the world, and insofar as they abide by the law they will be free to increase their wealth, property and scope of activity. Inequality is almost certain to flourish in these conditions, and it would not be deemed problematic within a state so organised. However, in other states, where more collective values hold sway, gross inequalities will be regarded as both problematic and undesirable. In reality, many Western nations, whilst accentuating the autonomy of the individual in recent years, still subscribe to some collective, or at least centralised, provision of certain 'basic' welfare services such as education, health and social security. The key point here is that the extent of equality or inequality will be affected by the extent of privilege and disadvantage permitted in a society, and these in turn will be affected by the aims of the principles in play as policy-making develops (Parsons, 1995; Wistow *et al.*, 1994; Bulmer *et al.*, 1989).

The individual or the environment? The focus for change

Finally, principles may shape policies which intervene at the level of the individual, or may change the structures and environments within which people live, or may have an impact on both the individual and the environment. In anarchic states individuals, up to the limits of their influence, bring about such changes as they wish. These changes may affect other people or may transform that part of an environment over which they exercise dominion. In more collectively-run states, however, joint decisions may determine whether a change must take place in individual behaviour or, alternatively, in the configuration of the (physical or social) environment. The question here is one of conformity. First, a state may have very strict and all-pervading laws with which individuals must comply, or alternatively a state may have very few, rather vaguely-drawn rules which allow individuals considerable liberty. In this latter case the only discipline may be of the self-imposed variety. But beyond the matter of external or internal authority, there is a further key question about the location of change. For any given set of circumstances, the question is whether it is the individual (or group) that must change (behaviour, attitudes, beliefs, etc.) or whether it is the (physical, social or political) environment that must be altered. We may see how critical will be the influence of prevailing principles in determining the focus for change.

Using the medical example once again, we may think of a health service that has the capacity to undertake 100,000 operations of a particular kind in any one year. However, let us suppose there are some 300,000 people on the waiting list for that operation. A principle that focuses on the individual may support a policy of rationing the treatment, reserving it only for those persons deemed to be in severest need. However, principles that focus on the context or environment may lead instead to policies which scrutinise the availability of services rather than evaluate the competing claims of users. Here, there may be a decision to allocate more resources and so increase the number of operations that could be performed each year.

Uniformity or diversity?

Many Western societies are increasingly multidimensional. They embody different communities, races, creeds and cultures. Within these states there are values and principles that we may call 'plural' inasmuch as they support and encourage diversity. But there are also values and principles that tend to the imposition of conformity or even uniformity. These we may call 'particular' or 'particularistic' principles. Here, diverse groups are invited or compelled to submit to the norms, ideologies and policies of the most powerful or dominant social, political and economic groupings (Lukes, 1974; Gramsci, 1971). In the remainder of the chapter I introduce some of the problems encountered in seeking either to reconcile these very different kinds of principle or, alternatively, in seeking to promote the one type over the other. My analysis is in four parts:

1. defining and contrasting plural and particularistic principles;
2. principles in conflict;
3. the mandate problem;
4. constraints on liberty.

Definition and contrast. I have said that principles may be drawn from, and support the values of, a particular group within some specified culture. Alternatively, they may recognise and accommodate diversity. These more 'open' or plural principles tend to be complex and harder to define. However, one way in which we may recognise policy principles which support diversity is that they will promote and adhere to equality of opportunity. In addition, principles designed to be sympathetic to the accommodation of diverse social groups may lead to policies which try to treat such groups even-handedly. For example, one aim may be to ensure that resources and services are distributed on the basis of 'substantive' criteria, that is, criteria intrinsic to the subject area of the policies concerned. So, for example, access to medical treatment would be determined by an individual's medical condition, rather than external factors such as his or her ethnic background or religious beliefs. Of course, there are thorny questions relating to the implementation of policy. Who is to decide what criteria are relevant in determining the allocation of resources in any given circumstance, and who is to measure citizens against these criteria in order to determine their priority for attention? Those who make these decisions may have their own prejudices and beliefs, or may even act corruptly. In some cases, therefore, plural principles might seem to prevail, but in reality they may be thwarted due to error or subversion at the organisational level. Our focus in this book is on *principles* rather than *practices* so that it may be helpful, perhaps, to set out side by side the properties of plural and particularistic principles. Accordingly, I describe the key differences between them in Table 2.2.

To summarise, the main difference between policies governed by particularistic and plural principles is to be found in their focus, composition and intention. Particularistic principles demand conformity to one set of prevailing values, whereas plural principles acknowledge and encourage a diversity of values and cultural norms. We should bear in mind that practice may enhance or subvert policy intentions.

By using the sorts of parameters set out in Table 2.2, it becomes possible to assess principles in terms of their effects on policy-making, and to understand the impacts of policies on citizens. There are, however, a number of problems inherent in the idea of pluralistic principles. Amongst the most important are: the existence of limits to the accommodation of diversity; the need to reconcile conflicting values; the problem of majority mandate; and, finally, effects that involve the constraint of individual liberties and freedoms.

Table 2.2   Criteria to distinguish between types of principles

	Particularistic principles	Plural principles
1. Policy intentions	Protect dominant values and the status quo	Allow for diversity and change
2. Basis of policy	Selectivity (rewards to those abiding by prevailing values, penalties for those who dissent)	Equality of opportunity, value relativity, conciliation of diverse cultures and groups
3. Policy purposes	Centralise, encourage conformity to prevailing values	Devolve power, give authority to individuals and local groups, encourage local and self-governance
4. Likely object of intervention	'Deviant' individuals and groups	The social and physical environment
5. Likely purpose of intervention	To change individual values and behaviours	To change social and physical environments
6. Effect on norms and values	Promote and reinforce prevailing norms	Respect differing norms and allow for diversity
7. Generic policy aims (might include)	To promote power-holders' interest, maintain prevailing norms and values, exclude competing principles, values and aims	To accommodate diversity and difference, recognize and allow, so far as is possible, competing values and aims

Principles in conflict. Values – embodied in principles – guide the creation of policy. One might therefore expect to find some measure of consistency between the various policies current in any particular society, irrespective of their specific purposes. This would be especially true where governments were unitary and strong. It would be incongruous (but not impossible) to discover opposing principles at play in localised or specific areas of policy. Only where the governance of a society was conducted by politically dissimilar entities at differing levels (for example central, regional and local authorities) would it be not at all unusual to see clashes of principle and, as a consequence, disagreement over policy. Ultimately, the severity of conflict within a system will determine its durability (and, finally, its viability).

I discuss diversity more fully in Chapter 6, but it is right to consider here the basic problem that there is a limit to the degree of diversity that any governing principles could accommodate. For example, it is hardly possible to pursue policies that aim both for equality and for privilege, or for ethnic equality as well as racial superiority. If principles come too fiercely into opposition, then either one principle will prevail over the other, or the society itself will shatter. After the break-up, the government of each new part will adopt the principles suited to them. There is, therefore, one respect in which a society which wishes to support pluralistic principles must be inflexible in its behaviour. Namely, a society must not allow pluralistic principles to be deposed by partial or particularistic ones, otherwise the ability to accommodate diversity and the desire to respect difference will be lost.

A further problem for a society which supports pluralistic principles is that of deciding criteria for action. In such a society there may be several value systems living side by side. Various groups will have differing beliefs, norms and priorities. In the light of these differing values and principles, how is a state to decide the criteria to be used in the elaboration of policy and the distribution of resources? One way of tackling this question would be devolution: to divide resources between each distinct group to allocate according to their own values and preferences (Bogdanor, 1979; Mackintosh, 1968). However, this approach runs the risk of allowing partial or particularistic principles to flourish as a consequence of the autonomy exercised by one segment or group within a society. A second method might be to search for criteria intrinsic to areas of policy. Consider, for example, the granting of bursaries for research into ancient scripts. A factor such as the colour of an applicant's eyes is hardly pertinent to awarding the grant, but expertise in ancient texts is clearly vital. Here, the decision-making criterion is substantive to the purpose. Moreover, this approach is sympathetic to the idea of equality of opportunity in that the position goes to the applicant most able to carry out the required duties. It may well be, therefore, that the defining quality of plural principles is that they are congruent with equality of opportunity. Conversely, partial or particularistic principles, those which support one sub-group of the population and one set of values only, will, in diverse societies, give rise to policies which may deny equality of opportunity. (I deal with questions concerning equality of opportunity in greater detail in Chapter 4.)

The 'mandate' problem. A further problem is that of 'mandate'. We have seen that plural principles value diversity, but it is the hallmark of a democracy that the will of the majority should prevail. Let us suppose a government received a democratic mandate gaining the votes of the large majority of the population. Let us also suppose that the manifesto of that government led to the adoption of certain policies which yielded privileges for that majority, very much to the detriment of various minority groups. The question is, are there any limits on what kinds of policy may be adopted in these circumstances? Can any sort of mandate be valid, even one that allows a government to pursue policies that differentiate between differing groups of citizens according to their ages, gender, disability, or ethnic origins, and so deny equality of opportunity?

Constraints on individual liberties and freedoms. In order to protect minorities and avoid injustices, there must be limits to the powers that majorities may enjoy. The reader may perhaps have surmised that plural principles are, therefore, prescriptive in at least one respect: they deny the legitimacy of differential citizenship. They forbid situations which would amount to the conferment on some of (unjust) privileges. In this way, plural principles delimit the boundaries of individual freedom. For example, I have said that under policies derived from constitutive or substantive criteria medical operations would be allocated, not according to any price list or scale of payment, but in response to medical need (I recognise that the definition of 'medical need' is, of itself, highly problematic). The objection may be raised that people should be free to choose how they wish to devote their resources, and to acquire a particular privilege (such as jumping the queue) if they so choose. But such a choice is only freely made where all *could* choose it. Where only some can make a choice, and others cannot, then as Lukes (1991: 50) has said 'freedom for the pike spells death for the minnows'.

A further objection may be raised that inequality of resources between people is actually fair, and that it is legitimate for people to be able to spend what they have earned in the way they wish. After all, some work harder than others and therefore rewards (incomes) *should* be unequal, there should be privileges (otherwise, why work harder?). It is thus entirely reasonable that some are able to choose more attractive options (such as jumping the queue) which lie out of the reach of others who didn't make similar efforts in their work.

One response might be that this scenario is fair if, and only if, (a) rewards and privileges are earned and distributed justly (for this to be true there can be neither inherited wealth nor luck, such as winning the national lottery), and (b) equality of opportunity applies in ensuring that all have the chance to make the effort and gain the same rewards and privileges for having made that effort. However, this still leaves the problem of a conflict between allocation of resources on the basis of need and the allocation of resources on the basis of (albeit earned) privilege (Freeman, 1999; Blakemore and Drake, 1996; Fishkin, 1983). This latter privilege is apparently reasonable in that it has been 'earned'. Without going into detail here, a brief answer might be that plural principles would permit individuals to make only those choices which flow from conditions of equality of opportunity. Policies derived from plural principles do not banish inequality, instead inequalities or differences between citizens arise fairly as a result of outcomes produced under conditions of equality of opportunity.

Difference and diversity can only take place within certain limits. There must be equality in terms of *potential* choice. Those freedoms or privileges which deny similar freedoms for others are, in the above context, unjust. For policy principles (and therefore policies themselves) to be fair, their prescriptions and effects must lie within such boundaries of action as to maintain equality in the *scope of freedom* available to all citizens. Another name for 'equality of scope' is *equality of opportunity*, and I deal with this concept in Chapter 4.

In this section I have introduced the notion of particularistic and plural principles. Particularistic principles lead to policies that support a political orthodoxy that reflects the values of one dominant party or group to the detriment or exclusion of others. Plural principles, on the other hand, accommodate a diversity of political values. However, I have argued that attempts at plurality may encounter a number of difficult problems. These could include the danger of social fragmentation, the dilemma of coping with majority mandates antagonistic to plurality, and the thorny matter of curtailing or removing some privileges and freedoms in order to optimise opportunity and to maximise scope for liberty across a diverse population as a whole. I discuss these issues in more detail later in the book and particularly in Chapter 6.

Conclusion

In this chapter I have been concerned with a number of crucial tasks. First, I have defined 'principle' as the link between values and policies. For policies to take shape they must have aims. Some goals will emerge from within the area to which a policy is applicable (substantive or constitutive aims), other objectives will have been drawn from the particular values at play, and will have general applicability beyond any single strand of policy. Second, I considered the purposes of principle. Specifically I argued that principles may be particularistic, supporting one value system, one set of norms, and, perhaps, one dominant group, to the subordination or exclusion of others. Alternatively, principles may be pluralistic, may accommodate more than one system of values, may conciliate various groups, recognise different cultures and respect diversity. Plural principles are congruent with the notion of equality of opportunity, but there are potential difficulties for diverse societies, even as far as the threat of actual break-up if values and norms clash too fiercely.

The scene is now set for us to consider certain principles which have proved resilient in Western democracies. In whatever policy areas we may nominate, time and again we come across claims by governments that their overarching principles are designed to protect liberty, ensure justice, achieve equity or fairness, respect diversity and secure citizenship. In the following chapters I scrutinise each of these in turn, starting in Chapter 3 with concepts of freedom and equality.

3

Freedom and Equality

According to its values and beliefs, a government may either fashion policies designed to intervene in society (for example to reduce levels of inequality or provide certain kinds of services) or, alternatively, it may adopt policies to avoid interference, reduce regulation, and (within bounds set by civil and criminal law) allow people to act much as they please, irrespective of outcomes such as greater levels of inequality and differential access to opportunities and privileges (Hill, 1997a,b; Farnham and Horton, 1996). Clearly, then, the principles used to shape any particular policy will *ceteris paribus* determine the kinds of impact it will have. Policies may either restrict the scope of individual liberty or, alternatively, may allow people such freedom of action as to widen the inequalities between themselves and others (Colebatch, 1998).

It is important to recognise difficulties in using concepts like liberty and equality in order to appreciate why questions of 'justice' or 'fairness' are so problematic. In this chapter, then, my first task is to explain how the concepts of liberty and equality have traditionally been understood. Second, I analyse the criticisms that have arisen of both egalitarianism and liberalism, and in particular I argue that, taken to their extremes, both freedom and equality are similarly despotic and tyrannical in their effects. I propose that absolute freedom for one entails enslavement of others, just as the absolute enforcement of equality for all results in choices for none because *choices involve differences* (Miller and Walzer, 1995; Kymlicka, 1989; Phillips, 1987). To reconcile (optimise) individual freedoms on the one hand, and communal equality (of consideration and treatment) on the other, some mechanism of mediation is needed, and I anticipate the next chapter by proposing that many writers have searched for such mediation through elaborating various concepts of *justice* and *fairness*.

43

Understandings of freedom

Many scholars agree with Cranston (1967) that the terms 'freedom' and 'liberty' are synonymous. Others, whilst not demurring, introduce distinctions of usage. For example, Gray (1991) comments that liberty is often used in a social sense (civil liberty) and freedom more often in an individual context (free will). Several writers have juxtaposed negative and positive aspects of freedom. So Milne (1968) and Cranston (1967) amongst others recognise that freedom requires an absence of external constraints or interference, but also involves the effective exercise of volition by an individual (freedom from x in order to do y). Other writers, however, have declared that we cannot define freedom simply in terms of individuals being free from external restraint. Indeed, theories of freedom which have descended from thinkers such as Marx and Rousseau emphasise the idea that liberty resides, at least in part, in some collective control over everyday life (Taylor, 1979). Rousseau (1762 [1968]), for example, held that a person was free when he or she was subject to laws imposed by him- or herself as a result of his or her participation in the formulation of society's collective view about what was just.

Yet others, such as Berlin (1969a) and Oakeshott (1975), refine our understanding of freedom by referring to the necessity that an individual must have the *capacity* to act as well as the *scope* to do so. An opportunity is not really an opportunity unless there is some feasible way of taking it. Feinberg (1980) has argued that what are thought to be bi-polar conceptualisations – of freedom *from* (external constraint) and freedom *to* – are not two different kinds of freedom at all; indeed any expression of liberty could be described from either point of view. To be free *to* sell newspapers is the same as to be free *from* being prevented from selling newspapers. Accordingly, these twin aspects of freedom have been resolved into a single expression by MacCallum (1967). MacCallum argues that freedom is not an absolute concept, but a relative one, residing in the formula 'X is free from Y to do Z'. Concurring in MacCallum's analysis, Gray (1991) argues that fragmented or partial understandings of freedom constitute *conceptualisations* of freedom, and that these constructions can differ markedly one from another in emphasis. It is this room for weighted emphasis that provides the focus here.

Our interest in the concept of freedom rests in its use by those who make social policy. Those with affinities to the right of the political spectrum tend to emphasise that part of the definition of freedom to do with the absence of constraint:

> Almost every post-war Tory victory had been won on slogans such as 'Britain Strong and Free' or 'Set the People Free, ... I was again asking the Conservative Party to put its faith in freedom and free markets (Thatcher, 1993: 7, 15).

The right does acknowledge the necessity of some governmental intervention in society, but its focus is less on the behaviour of companies and markets than on individuals. From this perspective, the demarcation of what is acceptable, and what is unacceptable, flows not so much from intervention in markets as from encouraging personal responsibility and adherence to traditional moral values:

> We were feeling our way towards a new ethos for welfare policy: one comprising the discouragement of state dependency and the encouragement of self-reliance; greater use of voluntary bodies including religious and charitable organisations like the Salvation Army, and, most controversially, built-in incentives towards decent and responsible behaviour (Thatcher, 1993: 629).

A further right-wing argument against intervention is economic. Minford (1991), Mount (1986), Friedman and Friedman (1980) and Hayek (1960) represent freedom in terms of the 'free market'. Accordingly, all these authors champion the cause of free trade and agree with Adam Smith's (1776) vision of government and, in particular, his view that the central and proper business of government was the protection of citizens (and markets) from coercion. These accounts are important not only for their theoretical contributions, but also because they inspired much New Right social and economic policy in the 1980s (Farnham and Horton, 1996; Clarke *et al.*, 1994). In sum, freedom of the individual is proposed on several grounds:

- that the exercise of free will is an essential part of being human;
- that freedom is a necessary factor in the progress of civilisation;
- that freedom to choose is a prerequisite of economic efficiency; and
- that freedom of the individual is a bulwark against the political tyranny of the left.

Those on the political left take a different view as to how freedom is secured. Many on the left assert that boundaries or limits must be placed on the scope of individual freedom in order, first, to prevent exploitation of others and, second, to promote some level of equality and some sense of collective interests:

> The aim of social justice is central to the Labour Party. There is no doubt that over the past few years the Party has moved towards a more favourable approach to the market, but it does, rightly, want to see it situated within a proper framework of values and to constrain some market outcomes. The project of the Left is to see individuals not only as consumers and producers, but as citizens acting together to ensure some common values and some common ends. We should be concerned with a wide range of outcomes: the distribution of power, the quality of social relationships, the quality of the environment and social or distributive justice which cannot be left to the short-term preferences of individuals in markets (Plant, 1993: 1).

From this perspective, deregulation across many areas of public and private enterprise is resisted because of its propensity to foster widening inequalities. Where deregulation occurs, some citizens can secure privileges at the cost of disadvantage for others (Alcock, 1996; Andrews and Jacobs, 1990; Lister, 1990). Here, then, the notion of 'freedom' is represented in terms very distinct from those common to the political right. Arendt (1968) has argued that a definition of liberty based only on a person's autonomy neglects the role of public institutions in safeguarding individuals from despotism. Similarly, Dahrendorf (1975: 5) contends that 'Friedman's obsession with the illiberal potential of government' leads him to underestimate the uncontrolled power of (allegedly) private organisations such as large companies or influential trade unions, whose actions may diminish the liberties of individuals outside these groupings. Secondly, Dahrendorf submits that the 'rearrangement' of life chances in education, work and leisure may require 'a redistribution of economic power which cannot be brought about by market forces alone'. We may trace these ideas at least as far back as Mill (1859), who counterposed the 'so-called liberty of the will' with 'civil, or social liberty' which he defined as the nature and limits of power which can be legitimately exercised by society over the individual. In similar vein, Jeremy Bentham (see Long 1977: 8) believed that the acquisition and maintenance of freedom required a 'logical and beneficial act', namely:

> the sacrifice of unrestricted but insecure liberties in return for a quantitatively circumscribed field of liberties which are secure and can be enjoyed ... Men thus seek, not to be free, but to possess a maximum of secure pleasure and to be assured of maximum protection against pain.

Galston (1991: 97) makes a similar point, but in doing so employs the notion of competing 'rights':

> Individuals who seek to exercise, without compromise, the totality of their presocial [*sic*] rights will quickly find that conflict with other rights-bearers impedes the attainment of their ends and the security of their liberty ... we are forced to conclude that public authority may legitimately restrict those rights in the name of maximising their effective exercise.

In this section of the chapter I have introduced the concept of freedom or liberty. MacCallum (1967) has provided an understanding of the concept as being in essence relative: 'X is free from Y to do Z'. In politics however, more partial conceptualisations have prevailed. On the right, the emphasis has been on freedom as the absence of external (especially governmental) interference, with boundaries, if any, self-imposed by personal subscription to traditional moral values. On the left, freedom has generally been defined in more collective terms with individuals ceding some measure of personal liberty in order to enjoy protection from coercion. As will be seen later in the book, which of these understandings is brought to bear can have a profound effect on the purposes and outcomes of social policies.

As a final point in this section, I should add that I will also be arguing that a truly free market as envisaged by New Right economists, a market in which each of the buyers and sellers commands influence over the market itself to an extent no greater than, and no less than, each of the others, is consonant with egalitarianism and social justice. I turn now, however, to the second major concept at the heart of this chapter: equality.

Understandings of equality and inequality

The concept of 'equality' has enjoyed widespread currency in political argument. To begin with, many egalitarian writers differentiate between two distinct uses of the term. First, 'equality' has been employed in a strict mathematical sense of two or more objects being identical to – or the same as – each other. Second, 'equality' has been used in a social and ethical sense, to the effect that individuals are entitled to equal treatment or consideration when their circumstances coincide.

Equality as an absolute is easy to imagine, but undesirable (and perhaps, impossible) to realise. If absolute equality prevailed, everybody would not only *have* the same, they would *be* the same. There could be no differences. Everyone would share identical attributes: the same physiology, the same abilities, energy, resources and aspirations. No distinctions could be discovered or made on any grounds. Where absolute equality prevailed, people would stand in circumstances identical one to another, would *be* identical one to another. Blackstone (1969: vi) describes such a state of affairs in these terms:

> A society without differences and, concomitantly, one without differential treatment of persons, would not only be boring, it would also be one in which the level of culture and civilization would be retarded and one which would result in great injustices.

As we will see in the next chapter, justice requires differential treatment of individuals according to differences in circumstance. Indeed, egalitarians protest against unequal treatment only when there are no rational grounds for it. Before we come to examine ideas of justice, however, we must understand the arguments on which those who have propounded equality base their case. There have been significant differences in approach.

The first thing to be said is that no serious egalitarian writers have made any demands for the introduction of the stark and unremitting version of absolute 'equality' that I described above. McCloskey (1966), Rees (1971), Turner (1986), Brown (1988) and many others have denied that a search for equality is an exercise in making people as like each other as possible. Indeed, not even Karl Marx (1938: 12) supported this absolute sense of the term, arguing instead that:

> the right of the producers is *proportional* to the labour they supply; the equality consists in the fact that measurement is made with an *equal standard*, ... this *equal* right is an unequal right for unequal labour. [original italics]

In similar vein, Engels wrote that 'the sort of socialism in which everyone received the same wages, the same quality of meat, the same quantity of bread, and received the same products in the same quantity – such a socialism is unknown to Marxism' (see Thomson, 1949: 8). Thomson concludes that no important political ideology with the possible exception of anarchism requires or demands abstract and absolute equality. In what ways, then, have egalitarians conceived of equality? A small minority have thought of equality in the sense of equalising income, but the overwhelming majority have stressed what we may call equality of treatment.

Perhaps Drabble (1988) took a position stronger than that of most egalitarians in wishing to see the establishment not only of equal rights, but also of equal pay and equal material goods. She took support in this desire from the arguments of George Bernard Shaw (1913). In a speech at the National Liberal Club, Shaw posed the following question: 'How are you going to give everybody in this room equal opportunities with me of writing plays? The fact is that you cannot equalise anything about human beings except their income'. Other writers, however, such as Crick (1992), Plant (1984) and the luminary in this field, R. H. Tawney (1964), have cast doubt on the viability of Shaw's standpoint. For example, Crick (1992: 3) wrote:

> Just suppose, imaginatively, that a benign iron regime imposed an exactly equal distribution of property and income; to keep it that way it would then have to legislate against any scope for the exercise of talent, greed or covetousness, against trading of any kind, against the buying or selling or swapping even, of personal possessions, and luck as well as lotteries would have to be abolished. This is abstract nonsense. Whoever believed in equality of result anyway?

Tawney (1964) has also attacked the notion of economic equality. His argument, he said, was *not* for the division of the nation's income into several million fragments, to be distributed without further ado, like a cake at a school treat, equally among all the families. Rather, it was to be achieved by using tax measures in order to pool surplus resources. These funds could then be used to make accessible to all so as to provide for each, irrespective of income, occupation, or social position, the conditions of civilisation which, 'in the absence of such measures, can be enjoyed only by the rich'. Tawney's aim, then, was to abolish what he called the 'most crushing of the disabilities and the most odious of the privileges'. Tawney sought practical and feasible movement towards equality and away from what he saw as excessive disparity, and the outcome he desired was the securing of 'a basic minimum below which none should fall', a minimum which would guarantee the essentials of civilised life. A more recent work by Baker (1987) added to the satisfaction of basic needs certain other ends considered by egalitarians to be desirable. Egalitarians believed that individuals were entitled to equal respect, political equality in the sense of participatory democracy, and equality of opportunity.

I have not yet examined the criticisms of equality made by right-wing thinkers, but some constraints have already been acknowledged by the concept's own supporters. To summarise these, the aim was not to bring about *sameness*. Most egalitarians concede not only that equal shares for all is a Utopian idea, but also that equal ability between people is simply not a reflection of real life. People have different skills, talents and amounts of determination, as well as different goals in life. Some work hard, others are lazy; some are serious, others happy-go-lucky; some adventurous, others cautious.

Second, egalitarians are not entirely agreed on the final outcome for which they are aiming. Some seek equality (or less disparity) of income between people. These writers want to see limits on wealth. Others are less concerned with the existence of unequal shares in the national cake, and strive more for equality of opportunity (see below). They envision a society in which opportunities are open for all to aspire to, and in which people are not handicapped by their skin colour, sex, religion or other factors which even today continue to give rise to prejudice (Bowie, 1988; Edwards, 1987; Florig, 1986). We see then, that there is a diversity of approaches amongst the supporters of equality which we may characterise as: equality of income, equality of treatment or consideration, equality of opportunity, and equality as individual fulfilment within society. As we will see, however, equality has critics who are against it *on principle*.

Some writers have objected to equality as being unattainable and not a feasible proposition. Letwin (1983) and Frankel (1971) have explored the conceptualisation of equality as being a fundamental consequence of the axiom that all human beings are members of a single reference group, the human race, and the conclusion that they are, therefore, entitled to equal treatment. Under this formulation, the *onus probandi* is shifted: whilst there is no need to justify equal treatment, instances of *unequal treatment* are to be scrutinised closely and must be justified by their proponents. Frankel contends that what follows from such a stance is the compulsion to redistribute wealth,

burdens and opportunities more equally. He objects to both assertions. First, he argues that there is no clear reason for 'equal shares'
to be a sort of 'default setting' or automatic choice in the absence of
reasons for differentiation. Second, he argues that some may not
want a portion of whatever it is that is being shared out, and may
want to swap for something else, even if the goods exchanged are of
unequal value. There may, however, be a non sequitur in Frankel's
analysis in that he conflates equal treatment (or a better term may be
'equal consideration') with equal shares. As we have seen, egalitarians accept that people may be treated *differently* but nevertheless
fairly, if the particular determining principle at work is a just one.
(Frankel recognises this fact, but seems not to allow it as being part
of the egalitarian position.)

If material resources are not to be divided equally, what of the problem of unequal skills? Berlin (1969b), for example, echoed Bernard
Shaw's objection that natural gifts and talents were unequally distributed amongst individuals, and pointed out that these differential aptitudes constituted a formidable obstacle to economic equality, because
in societies where there was a high degree of economic opportunity
the strong and able and ambitious and cunning were likely to acquire
more wealth or power than those who lacked these qualities. Berlin
also argued that for equality to be stable and persistent, everyone must
not only *have* the same, but must actually *be* the same, otherwise those
with ability and higher intelligence will soon place themselves in circumstances better than the norm and thus create or recreate inequality.
Somewhat tongue in cheek, Berlin suggested that in a society in which
absolute equality prevailed, certain phenomena could not exist, for
example the symphony orchestra in which every player used his or her
own interpretation of a piece, and his or her own tempo for its performance, would produce cacophony, rather than the harmony of sweet
music.

Following Berlin's analysis, Scruton (1982) has argued that to
maintain equality would require a constant process of redistribution
to prevent the growth of inequality. Such a system prefigures the
existence of a regulatory authority; either that or there must be no
systems of exchange at all. Both Berlin (1969b) and Scruton (1982)
concur, then, that absolute equality could only come about under the
supervision of a strict regulatory regime. However, Hayek (1960) has
asserted that any such supervisory mechanism must involve bureaucracy to such a degree that it would de facto interfere with and
diminish the liberty of the individual. Again, these objections are

based on the 'absolute' notion of equality rather than the idea of equal treatment.

But Hayek also attacked the notion of equality from a different angle. Accepting that people had differing talents and abilities, he argued that equality was incompatible with personal freedom. In Hayek's view, an individual should be free to save or expend his or her resources as he or she pleased. His argument was threefold. First, he proposed that there existed no generally accepted standard by which we can judge the justice or injustice of any particular distribution of wealth. For Hayek, an absolutely equal apportionment of resources might not, in itself, amount to a fair distribution of wealth, but, in any case, there was no way of knowing whether an equal distribution, or any specified unequal distribution, of resources was either fair or unfair, just or unjust. Moreover, there exists no independent or universal measuring device which would enable us to confirm or refute the rightness of any particular distribution of the world's resources.

Second, Hayek claimed that there are many possible definitions of justice and were a government to adopt and pursue only one of these definitions, disregarding all the others, then the preservation and promotion of the approved version must lead to a highly authoritarian state incompatible with personal freedom. Indeed, by these actions, even in seeking to create an equal society, a government which set store by one specific conception of what was fair would actually have no moral legitimacy. The goal of equality was therefore both illusory and unachievable.

Hayek brings together these two propositions, of there being no measuring device which would record whether a pattern of allocation was either just or unjust, and of there being no overriding or universal concept of justice, and he uses them in order to advance a third argument. In these circumstances, he says, there will be resentment from individuals and groups whose distributive share does not match their own view of what they deserve, their own view of what is just. The pursuit of equality creates unrealisable expectations which in turn create a crisis of legitimacy and authority. Hayek concludes, therefore, that government should confine itself to developing a framework of law that ensures that the processes of exchange are fair, but should not seek to redistribute wealth to achieve some believed or theoretical notion of social equality. The allocation of wealth should be left to the market; equality is neither a feasible, nor a legitimate aim for political action. Hayek's argument, then, was that the market should have free reign because imposed equality amounted to economic inefficiency and acted to the detriment of all. Furthermore, what was done in the name of social justice merely allowed one group or class to help itself from the pockets of another, and Hayek's fundamental point here was that the results of economic activity are not to be constrained by moral principles (Hayek, 1960).

The next step in Hayek's analysis was the argument that the goal of achieving equality (including an equal distribution of resources) was in fact an attempt to impose (non-economic) distributive criteria upon the market. The assumptions inherent in any such attempt are, first, that the activities of the market restrict freedom and cause injustice; and, second, that the market brings about circumstances in which the freedom of the poorest is restricted vis-à-vis the freedom of the better off. Hayek argued to the contrary, that economic transactions could not and do not have this degree of intentionality. Individuals make decisions about buying and selling in a plural market. It is this very plurality that ensures that a free market cannot be coercive, and the freedom of the poorest therefore cannot be diminished by their lack of resources. Accordingly, they have not suffered any injustice.

We see then that Hayek postulates a free market in which people are at liberty to trade and exchange as they wish. Some will win and some will lose, but the market itself has no intent: it cannot, as an entity, be malign, generous or anything else; the market is not, therefore, an oppressive mechanism. It is like the weather: some will go on holiday and get two weeks of sunshine, others will go another time and receive a fortnight of rain, but the weather itself has not 'decided' who will soak up the sun and who will be drenched. Of course, the acumen that people deploy in deciding when and where to go will improve or diminish their chances of good weather, but the weather itself has no intent one way or the other.

Hayek may well be right; it may well be true that a free market does not and cannot distribute wealth according to any particular set of moral principles. It may be, as he claims, that the outcomes of free markets are in principle *unprincipled*. In my own view, however, the analogy does not hold in real life: free markets, if they ever exist at all, seldom persist. They soon become *rigged* markets. From the start, those who are successful can use the advantage of their profits to move gradually towards dominance and then towards monopoly (see Walzer, 1983: 10–13), or they can form cartels and engage in price-fixing. In recent years, for example, smaller grocery shops in British town centres have suffered under the expansion of the out-of-town superstores. These gigantic supermarket chains wield enormous power in determining what people eat and how much they pay for it. If, through mergers and takeovers, a monopoly were to arise in an essential good, the controlling organisation could, as sole supplier, set artificially high prices for its products.

Clearly, then, though a market may not itself exhibit intentionality, those who operate within the market certainly do have intentions. And one aim may be to compromise the freedom of the market itself in order to gain an increasingly powerful position so as to outdo competitors and customers alike. Ultimately, the point is reached where, there being a lack of any constraint or regulation, monopoly can produce a situation in which the absolute liberty of the one (or the very few) entails the subordination, or even enslavement, of the many. I will return to this point later, but for now let us continue our review of the arguments against equality.

So far, then, objections have been raised in the name of practicality (that absolute equality is not a feasible aim), morality (that there is no way of knowing whether one distribution is to be wished over any other) and liberty (that the interventions required to secure equality constrain, and thus infringe, the liberty of individuals).

Joseph and Sumption (1979) offer further arguments. First, they attack the basis of support for equality as being emotional rather than rational. Egalitarianism, they say, is not a conclusion deduced logically from a premise. Rather, it is based, as all political premises are ultimately based, upon an emotional preference. Second, they propose that equality is destructive, and assert that 'brotherhood is destroyed by the abrasive measures which are required to make men equal'. They assume (p. 60) that where levelling takes place it will be downwards towards the lowest common denominator, rather than upwards towards the highest common factor. Third, they argue that inequality is necessary and ask: if equality of earnings prevails, who will do jobs that require long training, unpleasant conditions or rare intellectual application? We may perhaps note in passing that all too often people who do dirty or hazardous jobs are liable to receive very low pay, the 'incentive' argument for inequality is, to say the least, tenuous. Fourth, they assert, with Hayek and Scruton, that a rigorously logical approach to equality requires total levelling, the destruction of individual freedom and the erection of a totalitarian state to maintain that status quo. Finally, they speak in favour of inequality, arguing that such a state of affairs is not necessarily unjust. For Joseph and Sumption it is, rather, the imposition of total equality that is unjust. For them, equality is the equivalent of a rigged market.

In sum, then, absolute equality entails total uniformity and the absolute prevention of any inequality. But the achievement and maintenance of this state of affairs would demand a regulatory mechanism that would amount to despotic authority and the expunging of individual freedom. At the same time, however, extreme inequality may bring about absolute freedom and power for one ruler or for an elite leadership, but it would reduce the rest of the population to utter powerlessness and thus to slavery. So this state of affairs, too, amounts to despotic authority and the extinction of individual freedom. For different reasons, then, it would appear that both absolute equality and absolute inequality are the servants of tyranny. In both situations, liberty is extinguished for all but the tyrant, the elite, or the regulatory mechanism (call these things what you will). Must we therefore abandon both freedom and equality, or is it possible to achieve what Thomson (1969: 12) has described as 'liberty and equality reconciled and re-united'?

Equality of liberty

Egalitarians such as Thomson (1969) and Plant (1984) argue that the opponents of equality have been tilting at windmills, they have set up an Aunt Sally, they are attacking a straw horse. What they have criticised is their own misrepresentation of equality. Plant (1984) points out that egalitarian authors accept that the notion of absolute, total and unremitting equality in human affairs is absurd. Such a goal is not, and has never been their aim. Plant advances three key rebuttals.

In the first place, it matters not whether a market, free or otherwise, causes or does not cause inequality. What matters, is how we respond to inequality. Justice and injustice are matters of our attitudes and if we (a society or community) perceive something as being unjust, we can ameliorate it, no matter how it was caused in the first place. Second, the liberal view of freedom as set forth in the works of (*inter alia*) Hayek, Friedman and Minford is based on negatives, such as the absence of coercion or the avoidance of taxes intended to raise funds for the benefit of others. But egalitarians claim that there are also positive representations of liberty, such as the freedom to work or the freedom to participate in political debate and decision-making. In the end, liberty depends on having sufficient economic and social resources in order to exercise choice. If there is no choice, there can be no liberty. Indeed, it may be argued that the magnitude of a person's liberty is to be measured in the scope or extent of his or her possible choices. As Tawney (1964: 228) has argued:

> [freedom means] the ability to do, or refrain from doing definite things, at a definite moment, in definite circumstances, or it means nothing at all.

In the third strand of Plant's rebuttal, he repeats the point made earlier in the chapter, that egalitarians do not aspire to impose a uniform pattern of life, they are not the harbingers of unremitting and monotonous sameness. Rather, they are concerned with equality of consideration and equality of opportunity. Accordingly, in his definition of equality, Laski (1969) nominates three key components:

1. the absence of special privilege;
2. the adequacy of opportunities open to all; and,
3. up to the margin of sufficiency, an identity of response to primary needs.

The sense of equality as equal treatment has been prominent in constitutional history. For example, the French Declaration of Rights in 1789 avowed 'Men are born and remain free and equal in rights' and the law should:

> be the same to all, whether it punishes or protects; and all being equal in its sight are equally eligible for all honours, places and employments according to their different abilities, without any distinction than that created by their virtues and talents.

Finally, perhaps Crick (1992: 3, 4) has most cogently summarised the mainstream egalitarian position in arguing that:

> Equality must be rooted in how we treat each other as persons, in whether we genuinely see all others as equals, as of equality of worth, ... equality as a value or a standard of conduct could and should govern most aspects of our lives ... Equality and liberty are in perpetual tension, but one can never extinguish the other utterly without destroying our basic humanity as well.

Egalitarians complain that the assault on equality launched by libertarians is an attack on a position they (the egalitarians) do not hold.

In their turn, libertarians, such as Taylor (1979), complain that supporters of equality attack meanings of liberty (such as the freedom to be despotic) that were never intended by its adherents. So, for example, Joseph and Sumption (1979) define freedom as the absence of coercion or constraint but add that liberty may be exercised only 'without encroaching on the freedoms of others' (p. 49). Again they assert that a person is morally entitled to make acquisitions *except* through monopoly, force or fraud (p. 76). Similarly, Berlin (1969a: 170) has argued that the extent of people's liberty to choose:

> to live as they desire must be weighed against the claims of many other values, of which equality, or justice, or happiness, or security, or public order are perhaps the most obvious examples. For this reason it cannot be unlimited.

In seeking to transpose these academic ideas into political practice, Tebbit (1986: 3) has argued:

> Freedom without self-restraint degenerates into licence and inevitably and quickly leads to the abrogation and denial of the freedoms of others. To help instil that sense of responsibility and to give it direction, we Conservatives look now, as in the past, to traditional values and standards of decency and order – in social just as in economic affairs.

Neither libertarians nor egalitarians assert or desire the bringing about of freedom or equality in their absolute or unconstrained manifestations. In the heat of political debate, the adherents of both ideologies profess themselves to be against restrictive practices. The targets for egalitarians include the old boy network, freemasonry, and the gentlemen's club. Libertarians, on the other hand, demonise the trade union chapel and the closed shop. All these have in common that they provide certain privileges and life chances for some, whilst denying those same opportunities to others.

This brings us to what may seem at first sight a startling proposition: that both egalitarians and libertarians support *equality of liberty*. The free market, beloved of libertarians, is the economic equivalent of the equality of opportunity sought by egalitarians. How can this be? Put simply, where egalitarians subscribe, not to the absolute or mathematical sense of equality in the sense of all people standing in identical circumstances, but to equality of opportunity in the sense of social, economic and political inclusion, in people having equal chances to develop their skills and capacities to pursue legitimate dreams and objectives, in there being open access and fair tests for positions and offices, then they actually support the notion of *the free market*. A free market is one in which no participant is able to fix supply or demand, no participant can corner the market or acquire special advantages or privileges. Certainly people will make different choices, will have differing aims, and these differences may be called 'inequalities'. But in a free market, opportunities will exist for all participants. It is rational to believe that choices will be made in pursuit of fulfilling their wishes and their potential. This is precisely how Baker (1987: 49) perceives equality of opportunity and the goal of egalitarianism:

> The truly egalitarian attitude towards opportunity is to give everyone the means to develop their capacities in a satisfying way, [this] requires a restructuring which really does try to match social roles to individual capacities.

The critical point here is that in a truly free market, people may trade voluntarily and openly between each other. There are no restrictions, cartels or monopolies to prevent the transfer of goods or engage in price-fixing. No buyer or seller is in a position to coerce or compel any other into any particular contract, or strong enough to prevent two other persons entering freely into a contract if they so wish. Buyers and sellers are free to make their own decisions according to their needs, wants and interests. This same vision may be applied in a social rather than an economic sense.

One component of social policy analysis is the detection of purpose. From the discussion so far we see that there may be a spectrum of general aims for social policies. First, some governments may produce policies designed to maximise individual liberty irrespective of unequal outcomes. Alternatively, policies may be designed to achieve a redistribution of resources in order to bring about a greater measure of equality, but in so doing the scope of liberty may, for some citizens, be reduced (for example through taxation and the consequent reduction of purchasing power). Third, policies may be aimed at equalising, not material resources, but the scope of liberty and opportunity available to each citizen. Relating these points to the discussion of plural and particularistic principles in Chapter 2, we may see that where a society is diverse, plural principles will be more sympathetic to egalitarian notions, whereas particularistic principles may be more the product of libertarian regimes.

Again using the example I explored in Chapter 2, let us imagine a government intent on an education policy based on absolute equality. Our vision runs into trouble almost at once. Every pupil must be taught the same subjects, in an identical way, to the same standards, each must be expected to attain the same level of achievement irrespective of the interests, talents and aptitudes of each. This is patent nonsense. But so would be a policy based on absolute individual freedom. Since no one has to pay tax, where does the money come from to build schools? If not in schools, where and how are pupils taught, and by whom? What happens if they do not wish to learn anything? What happens if they wish to learn something that no other individual wishes to teach? An education policy based on 'equality of liberty' (see, for example, Baker, 1987) seems far more practicable, in that it presages the development of a variety of types of educational enterprises able to focus teaching on the differing strengths and potential of individuals. Access to these 'schools' might be self-elective rather than decided by factors external to education such as parental wealth.

Conclusion

In this chapter, I have reviewed the concepts of 'equality' and 'liberty'. Not only are they disputed ideas, but political and academic debate has been clouded further by egalitarians and libertarians sometimes misrepresenting each other's position. I suggested that there was some common ground between the two extremes expressed by the notion of 'equality of liberty'. Applying these ideas to policy creation, it was clear that a radical libertarian position would heavily restrict the scope of government to intervene in society against inequality. Similarly, an extreme egalitarian position would produce policy which might equalise material resources but diminish individual liberty. I have mooted the possibility that there may be a point of balance between individual freedom and communal equality in the idea of 'equality of liberty'. At first sight, the mechanisms for discovering and maintaining such a balance are *justice* (*fairness*) and *equality of opportunity*, and it is to these concepts that I now turn.

4

Concepts of Justice and Equality of Opportunity

In the previous chapter I argued that in real life neither egalitarians nor libertarians press their respective causes to the absolute. By recognising the undesirability (indeed, impossibility) of either total equality or wholly unconstrained liberty, we are brought to the key questions: where lies the balance between liberty and constraint, between equality and inequality? How are we to decide what is fair? This question of justice is as appropriate to social policies as it is to other areas of governance. However, there is no agreement about the meaning of the term 'justice' itself. In this chapter I deal with four very different attempts at conceptualising justice: justice as utility; justice as entitlement; justice as contract; and finally a non-universal conceptualisation, 'spheres' of justice.

I begin with the utilitarian ideas of Mill (1859) and Bentham (1780, 1776) before moving to the 'entitlement' notion of justice as advanced primarily by Nozick (1974) and Hayek (1960) (justice as applied to the *processes* of interaction and exchange as opposed to their *outcomes*). Next I contrast Nozick's view with the contractual understanding of justice elaborated by Rawls (1972), from which perspective justice must deal as much with ultimate outcomes (i.e. particular distributions of social goods) as with the fairness of the interactions and exchanges that led to those outcomes. Finally, I assess a model of justice that rejects the universal claims of all these previous accounts. For Walzer (1983), the very plurality and diversity of life precludes the possibility of enunciating some single, abstract formulation of justice. Instead, he argues that in each different sphere of social intercourse a different definition of justice will emerge, drawing on differing criteria from within each sphere.

The final part of the chapter is devoted to further analysis of 'equality of opportunity', an equally contentious concept that stands at the heart of Rawls's understanding of 'fair inequalities'.

Justice as utility

John Stuart Mill (1859) attempted to define 'justice' by proposing that it was to be found in whatever decisions or actions produced the most good. Both Mill and Bentham (1780, 1776) argued that the aim of life was happiness, and the yardstick was calibrated in pleasure and pain. Justice amounted to the greatest good of the greatest number. At first sight this appears to be an eminently sensible, simple and workable concept. There were, however, stumbling blocks. In applying Mill's formulation, it was possible to conceive of particular conditions in which gross injustices were perpetrated on individuals for the sake of the rest of the community. Lebacqz (1986) illustrated this point with the example of the scapegoat, the death of an innocent member of a group in order that the rest of that community be preserved.

However, Mill had recognised and countered such objections. He postulated a number of specific kinds of circumstance which amounted to, or produced, injustice, and which must override the more general rule. The circumstances nominated were to include depriving people of things to which they were legally or morally entitled, or depriving them of things they deserved, breaking faith with people and being partial or treating people unequally when they deserved to be treated equally with their peers. The scapegoat example clearly amounts to an injustice under several of these headings. Mill unifies these various types of injustice using the notion of breaking *duties* or *perfect obligations*. For Mill, perfect obligations generate *rights* which would be denied wherever such injustices occurred (Stevens, 1982; Cowling, 1963).

This utilitarian concept of justice recognises that individuals' rights must be supported by society as a whole because such rights apply to all individuals; accordingly the idea of equal treatment is also supported. The notion of the greatest good of the greatest number is thus sustained at the macro-level, even if the idea is sometimes (necessarily) compromised at the micro-level, where, through the exercise of a right, an individual's good may be so important as to transgress any simple calculation concerning the general good. In any case, it may be that the denial of a right held by one individual in a particular circumstance may, in setting a precedent, threaten the same right for all other individuals. In the end, such a transgression would not produce the greatest good of the greatest number after all. If justice does not equate straightforwardly with maximising good, may we be any more successful in conceptualising justice as an entitlement?

Justice as entitlement

A second kind of analysis is offered by Nozick (1974), who proposes an entitlement theory of justice. The theory is based on three principles: justice in acquisition, justice in transfer, and justice in rectification. Wolff (1991) argues that Nozick did not make clear his notion of justice in acquisition, but perhaps the nearest we can come to an understanding of what was intended is that an act of appropriation (property acquisition) is justified if and only if it makes no one worse off. Nozick accepts (albeit in a weakened form) what is called the *Lockean proviso*. The Lockean proviso holds that an acquisition is allowable, *provided* that other persons are not prevented from making a similar acquisition (see Lebacqz, 1986: 57). The essential point here is that acquisitions are unjust if they result in the creation of a monopoly. The second principle put forward by Nozick was that transfers (transactions or exchanges) are only justifiable if they are voluntary, and here again the Lockean proviso would apply. Voluntary transfers are just only where they do not prevent others from making similar voluntary transfers. The third principle, justice in rectification, involves putting right circumstances constituting injustices under the first two principles.

As with Mill, there are problems with Nozick's attempt at defining justice. With regard to the first principle (justice in acquisition), it is difficult to define 'worse off'. How are we to know, asks Wolff (1991), whether a particular acquisition has left others worse off by their not being able to make an identical acquisition? And as to the second principle, whether a transfer was voluntary or not will depend not only on whether there was coercion surrounding the immediate circumstances of the transfer, but also whether there were alternative choices available to each participant. Did a lack of options actually compel an ostensibly voluntary transfer? A key criticism of the third principle (justice in rectification) is that of practicality: how far back into history can one go in order to put right previous injustices?

Nozick's conceptualisation of justice amounts to this. In his view justice applies far more to the conduct of transactions than to their consequences. Apart from the prevention of monopoly and the prevention of violence, Nozick believes that outcomes do not fall within the purview of justice. By and large it is only processes, not effects, that should be subject to the demands of justice. Nozick's viewpoint follows from his belief, first, that individuals are entitled to own private property, second, that they are entitled to make 'voluntary transfers' of that property to others, and, third, that the intervention of the state should be heavily restricted. Accordingly, in Nozick's view, the legitimate roles of the state are limited to ensuring fair processes of exchange and providing compensation when certain liberties are restricted by the state itself in order to protect 'fundamental rights'. (For example, Nozick sees the state as holding a monopoly of force in order to prevent aggression by individuals. Such aggression would transgress the fundamental right of individuals not to be assaulted or killed.) We can see why it is that Nozick's view of the role of government has been called the 'minimal state'. Allowable interference is kept to a minimum. For Nozick, as long as initial acquisition and subsequent transactions arise fairly, it matters not how great the inequalities that might ensue as a result. Inequalities are just where they arise through fair means from an initially just situation (Lebacqz, 1986: 55).

Some of the key implications of Nozick's position are explored later in the book, but it might be said, in passing, that they can be surprising. For example, he regards taxation as theft. For Nozick, any 'patterned principles' of (re-)distributive justice (such as compulsory National Insurance contributions and the payment of social security benefits) inevitably violate people's (in this example, contributors') rights. By 'right' Nozick means the right *voluntarily* to conduct transactions within a fair process (Norman, 1987). Those who believe that justice must apply as much to outcomes as to processes regard Nozick's theory as wholly inadequate. These writers turn instead to thinkers like John Rawls, who proposes a contractarian model of justice.

Justice as contract

In his *Theory of Justice*, John Rawls (1972: 302) was concerned about consequences as well as processes. He developed two fundamental principles of justice:

First Principle
Each person is to have an equal right to the most extensive total system of equal basic liberties compatible with a similar liberty for all.

Second Principle

Social and economic inequalities are to be arranged so that they are both:

(a) to the greatest benefit of the least advantaged, consistent with the just savings principle, and

(b) attached to offices and positions open to all under conditions of fair equality of opportunity.

(The 'just savings' principle need not detain us here, but is concerned with the question of fairness over time and between generations. See Rawls, 1972: 284–302.) The first principle, which prescribes equality of liberty, may be represented in a diagrammatic form. Figure 4.1 sets out a position to represent the most extensive total system of equal basic liberties compatible with a similar liberty for all.

The second diagram (Figure 4.2) shows a position in which the system of liberties is unequal and thus contravenes Rawls's first principle. Here, the liberty being exercised by person 'A' compromises or usurps the liberty of others by limiting the scope or choices available to them.

With his second principle, Rawls attempts to define the circumstances in which certain types of inequality are justifiable. He contends that inequalities are just where they are (a) arranged to the greatest benefit of the least advantaged, and (b) where the inequalities are not *personal* privileges, but are instead attached to offices and positions open to all under conditions of fair equality of opportunity.

As it was with Nozick, so too with Rawls: a number of criticisms have been levelled at the theory. First, there is a question of practicability.

B	C	D
E	**A**	F
G	H	I

Figure 4.1   The extent of liberty available to A is equal to that available to neighbours B, C, D, E, F, G, H and I

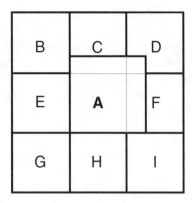

Figure 4.2   The extent of liberty exercised by A is so great that it
infringes the liberty of neighbours C, D and F

As Wolff (1977: 195–210) explains, principle 2(a) (known as the
difference principle) is quite difficult to get to grips with. How are we
to tell which particular distribution of inequalities would most benefit
the least advantaged? There are any number of different ways of
organising society in order to produce goods and services and:

> the manifest vagueness of these calculations and estimations has a very
> important consequence for Rawls's theory. Inevitably, one finds oneself
> construing the difference principle as a pure distribution principle.

Second, there are problems of definition. Rawls argues in principle
2(b) that it should be open to all of us to aspire to positions (offices)
under conditions of fair equality of opportunity. As we will see later
in the chapter, the notion of equality of opportunity is a highly contested one, having its own problems of definition and application.

Third, Kukathas and Pettit (1990) challenge the basis of the principles themselves. Rawls developed the principles by imagining that a
population had to design the society in which they were going to live
'behind a veil of ignorance'. That is, no person knew the position he
or she would occupy in society until *after* the rules had been agreed.
Given rational choices, what would be the result of their delibera-
tions? Rawls argued that because no one knew whether they would be
well situated or badly off in the social structure, most would be likely
to display a conservative attitude, choosing an option that offered the

least worst outcome (to guard against the ill-fortune of being in the worst position). However, Kukathas and Pettit (1990) point out that human beings may be more adventurous than Rawls allows; they may be ready to risk choosing a society where the best and worst placed are far more divergent than under Rawls's conception. In this case, the principles of justice would be much nearer to Nozick's account. Inequality would not be constrained by considerations of fair outcomes.

I am conscious of treating the work of Mill, Nozick and Rawls with a brevity bordering on the disrespectful. However, there are very many texts devoted solely to the thinking of each of these luminaries, and our purpose here is to employ these broad but divergent ideas about justice in order to throw light on the principles that stand behind contemporary social policies. In particular, we may contrast Nozick's view of 'justice as entitlement' with Rawls's view of 'justice as fairness'. It is immediately apparent that the state has much more to do where Rawls's justice prevails than it has under Nozick's auspices.

There are, however, heavy criticisms made of Rawls's abstract approach in attempting to determine the meaning of justice. For example, Young (1990: 4) argues that where a theory of justice:

> is truly universal and independent, presupposing no particular social situations, institutions or practices, then it is simply too abstract to be useful in evaluating actual institutions and practices. In order to be a useful measure of actual justice and injustice, it must contain some substantive premises about social life, which are usually derived, explicitly or implicitly, from the actual social context in which theorizing takes place.

Young (p. 4) contends that rather than seeking some systematic theory of justice, our task is to 'clarify the meaning of concepts and issues, to describe and explain social relations, and articulate and defend ideals and principles'. For her, 'normative reflection begins from historically specific circumstances'. It is just such an approach that has been adopted by Will Kymlicka and (separately) Michael Walzer, to whom we now turn.

'Spheres' of justice

In his seminal work on political philosophy, Will Kymlicka (1990: 1) argues that the traditional way of thinking about political principles is that they 'fall somewhere on a single line stretching from left to right'. Moreover, those on the left favour equality (and thus support socialism) whilst those on the right eulogise freedom (and the free market). For Kymlicka, like Young, this view fails to reflect a more complex reality. Left and right have views about fairness and justice in government and the economy, but what about other spheres such as domestic life? Kymlicka, Young and Walzer all come to the view that the enterprise of seeking out 'one true theory of justice seems wholly implausible'.

These theorists argue that justice cannot be found through abstract cogitation, but rather, definitions of justice are created in a living way within differentiated cultures and unique spheres of social life. This view is close to that of communitarian thought:

> Communitarians believe that evaluating political institutions cannot be a matter of judging them against some independent ahistorical standard ... political judgement is a matter of interpreting the traditions and practices we already find ourselves in. So there are issues of 'embeddedness' which are not addressed in left–right debates (Kymlicka, 1990: 2).

In passing, Kymlicka concludes from this that we cannot understand feminism or communitarianism if we insist on locating them somewhere on a left–right political spectrum (see also Hughes, 1996). But the importance of Kymlicka's thinking in the present context is that he is suggesting that neither can we locate some overarching definition of justice in that way either.

> The left can argue that if you believe in equality then you should support socialism; and the right can argue that if you believe in freedom, you should support capitalism. But there is no way to argue for freedom over equality or equality over freedom, since these are foundational values, with no higher value or premiss that both sides can appeal to ... we are left with nothing but conflicting appeals to ultimate, and ultimately opposed, values (Kymlicka, 1990: 3).

Kymlicka adds to these old values of equality and liberty, appeals to newer ultimate values, 'contractual agreement' (Rawls); rights (Dworkin) or 'androgyny' (feminism). But, he continues, 'this explosion of potential ultimate values raises an obvious problem for the whole project of developing a single comprehensive theory of justice. Without such a deeper value there could only be ad hoc and localised resolutions of conflicts.'

However, Kymlicka (1990) and Dworkin (1977) agree that which-
ever of these values is in play, all of them concur in the notion that
each person matters equally in all plausible political theories, and
this notion that each person 'signifies' is also crucial to Walzer's theory
of justice.

Walzer's (1983) theory opposes the notion that some abstract conceptualisation of justice can be developed which is then applicable in
all aspects of life. Instead, Walzer elaborates what Miller (1995: 2)
has called a radically pluralistic account. Within Walzer's account
there are no universal laws of justice. Instead we must see justice as
being defined by a particular community at a particular time. In this
way specific definitions of justice emerge from within communities,
not from outside them.

Walzer argues that there are within a society various types of 'social
goods' (money, status, property, honour, and so forth) and that different
distributive criteria may apply to different types of goods. (That the
allocation of different social goods may occur on entirely different
bases, one from another.) Accordingly, the presence or absence of justice in each of these spheres of life is to be judged using different criteria in each and every case. As Miller (1995) contends, there is no
underlying principle to be found standing behind all these distributive
criteria which arise from within communities themselves.

So, whereas in their search for definitions of justice, Rawls and
earlier theorists seek some abstract and external formula which may
subsequently be imposed on social structures and transactions, Walzer
argues that varieties of definitions of justice emerge from within
social structures and transactions and these definitions are specific to
each sphere of living. There is, says Miller (1995), no core idea which
might explain why some things are to be distributed in one way and
other things in another.

It may be that Walzer's account more accurately describes the reality of everyday living, in which different people hold different ideas
about what constitutes justice in various spheres of life. However,
Walzer's analysis seems more concerned with how people arrive at,
and use, various definitions of what they label 'justice'. Rawls, it
seems to me, is undertaking a different task. For him the key question
is: how are we to know whether something is fair ('just') or not, irrespective of whether some social group or population claims that it is?

Despite this seeming anarchy, Walzer does make one general claim
about this distributive pluralism, namely, that it leads to complex
equality. Put simply, people may benefit from a definition of justice at

play in one sphere of life, but fare badly under another set of distributive criteria in some other. However, it is not possible to convert an advantage in one sphere into an advantage in others. What prevails is 'complex equality' by which is meant a balancing out of injustices leading to a general condition of fairness. However, Young (1990) resists the idea that what emerges from individual inequalities is an overall complex equality. She argues (in concurrence with Lukes, 1974) that where one group comes to dominate many spheres the outcome is injustice in the shape of (structural) oppression. Young (1990: 48–62) nominates five criteria for determining the existence or otherwise of oppression. These are: exploitation; marginalisation; powerlessness; cultural imperialism; and violence.

Exploitation consists in a 'steady process of the transfer of the results of the labour of one social group to benefit another'. Marginalisation occurs to those people whose labour a system cannot use. Groups are powerless where they are unable to amend the structures that impose exploitation and marginalisation:

> Domination in modern society is enacted through the widely dispersed powers of many agents mediating the decisions of others. To that extent many people have some power in relation to others, even though they lack the power to decide policies or results. The powerless are those who lack authority or power even in this mediated sense (Young, 1990: 56).

Accordingly, cultural imperialism occurs when dominant social meanings 'render the particular perspective of one's own group invisible at the same time as they stereotype one's group and mark it out as 'The Other' (Young, 1990: 58). One consequence of such stereotyping is the risk of suffering violence at the hands of 'mainstream' society. This analysis leads Young (1990: 39) to conclude that 'justice' must refer not only to distributive criteria but also to institutional conditions, particularly those necessary 'for the development and exercise of individual capacities and collective communication and cooperation'.

Barrett and Phillips (1992) develop a feminist argument against general theories, be they of 'justice' or any other pivotal social concepts. Phillips (1992: 11) summons the work of MacIntyre (1988, 1981) and Rorty (1989) in aid of her contention that notions of reason, morality and justice are 'grounded in historical traditions', but that we need to move away from 'Enlightenment tradition and towards a new emphasis on heterogeneity, diversity and difference'.

Phillips concurs with Pateman's (1989, 1988) view that citizenship 'has been made in the male image' with the result that justice is defined in terms of fair contract and exchange in which anything (including our own bodies) can be bought and sold. 'Applied to women, this justifies prostitution'. Phillips (1992: 12) rehearses Pateman's argument that:

> Those who seek to deny the body, who deal only in the abstraction of 'the individual' or 'the citizen', who think it should make no difference whether these individuals are women or men, will be writing in one sex alone as their standard. Women can be encompassed on an equality with men only if sexual difference is first of all acknowledged.

Perhaps the key point here is that for Phillips any theory of justice must take into account multiple differences between, for example, men and women, disabled and non-disabled, black and white, young and old, and the 'tendency towards universalism' which subsumes and then ignores these differences within terms like 'citizen' and 'individual' should be firmly resisted. We may compare this view – that justice must allow for differences between people – with Walzer's view that justice must be tested for differently in different spheres of life.

Indeed, Phillips (1992: 14) recognises the link when she says:

> attention has shifted from establishing universally applicable standards of morality and justice towards elucidating the principles that are already present within any given society. The result is, to use Michael Walzer's words, 'radically pluralist'. Notions of justice are said to exist already as a part of a community's shared intuitive beliefs, but they are often hidden or latent ... however, because they are grounded in the particular history of a specific community they cannot claim any universal relevance or scope.

These ideas are congruent with Rorty's (1989) view that people sympathise notwithstanding differences between them, rather than as a result of some basic shared humanity. Phillips thus concludes that our beliefs are not universal, but 'local, particular and contingent'.

How then, in her view, may equality and justice be achieved? Phillips recognises that in the actuality of everyday life there is a conflict or dilemma between those who argue that justice is to be found in equality (of consideration or treatment) and those who believe justice to be grounded in difference. Phillips (1992: 20) argues that there are multiple differences, between men and men, and between women and women, as well as between men and women. Indeed, there are 'seemingly endless differences' when we consider race, disability and so forth. How is it possible to think of universal meanings of justice and equality if people are so diverse? Ultimately Phillips comes to a hybrid answer. First, she accepts Eisenstein's (1989) argument that equality must encompass generalisation, abstraction and homogeneity as well as individuality, specificity and heterogeneity. Phillips (pp. 20–3) agrees that some transcendency is needed in order to understand what human beings have in common as well as what separates them, but rejects the view that this necessitates a unitary standard against which all are judged. Instead 'the notion of a unitary standard which is then varied in its applications is not such a novel idea'. In particular she concurs with Young's view that there must be mechanisms to represent the voices and perspectives of oppressed groups, but recognises (p. 27) that this need is symbolic of an 'impulse towards universality, a recognition of the partial, and potentially confining, nature of all our different and specific identities, a commitment to … a politics of greater generality and alliance'. But she insists that this is not to be a 'fruitless pursuit of a genuinely de-gendered universal'. I am reminded here of Aristotle's dictum that it is unjust to treat equals differently or unequals the same.

To summarise, Phillips contends that because 'justice' is a social artifact, no universal theory is possible *in lived reality*. When claims of universality are made for particular conceptualisations of justice, they are subsequently shown to be definitions provided by powerful groups who, through their power, can bring such definitions, either voluntary or through imposition, to more general acceptance.

Comparing theories of justice

I have introduced four conceptualisations of justice: as utility, as entitlement, as contract, and as a specific artifact unique to each sphere or aspect of life in each distinctive culture which must respond differently to people as they are different from each other. Each account offered its own way of locating two balancing points.

First, there is a balance to be struck between the extent of liberty that any individual (or group) may enjoy and the degree of constraint a state may impose to protect the freedoms of other individuals. Second, a point of balance is sought between the freedom of an individual (or group) to acquire resources (property, wealth, influence and power) and the imposition of limits to the extent of such inequality in order to prevent the exploitation of human beings that monopoly (or tyranny) may bring. If justice is *only* about ensuring fair processes then an individual's freedom to acquire is absolute (or almost absolute), and exploitation becomes acceptable even to the point of infringing the liberties of others (as in Figure 4.2). If justice is concerned with outcomes as well as processes (ensuring fair processes *and* limiting the extent of inequality) then the scope of the liberty available to an individual is bounded; in particular it falls short of the infringement of the liberty of others (as in Figure 4.1). But how are we to decide which of these (or any other) concepts of justice to adopt? The many possible understandings of justice are based on starkly differing rationales and they have led MacIntyre to ask: 'Whose Justice? Which Rationality?' As MacIntyre (1996: 1) asserts:

> some conceptions of justice make the concept of desert central, while others deny it any relevance. Some conceptions appeal to inalienable human rights, others to some notion of social contract, and others again to a standard of utility.

MacIntyre contends that what people do in practice is to give their allegiance to 'rival traditions of enquiry' and there are 'no tradition-independent standards of argument by appeal to which they can be shown to be in error'. As a result, different notions of 'justice' prevail in different societies which are themselves held together by different systems of rationality. Plant (1990: 11) agrees with McIntyre's analysis, but goes further, arguing that within:

> a morally pluralist society we have no way of coming to some objective agreement about the various contending criteria of social justice. These may be, for example, distribution according to need, desert, merit, or entitlement; utilising these different criteria will yield different distributions of resources. However, in the view of the neo-liberal, given moral pluralism, we have no way of reaching agreement on the priority of the different criteria. On this view there is no consensual account of what needs are, or of what merit and desert consist. These will differ according to different moral frameworks.

Plant concludes that due to the lack of agreed standards, it is not possible – once and for all – to define justice (he uses the term 'social justice'), leaving the field open for various interest groups to press for their own 'inherently disputable demands'. What, then, are we to do? How may we discuss the principles of social policy if they are built on the shifting sands of conceptual mutability?

Though the conceptual models of justice I have introduced here seem very different, how different would be the worlds they might produce in practice? Neither Mill nor Rawls proscribes inequality, each merely emphasises that inequalities should be beneficial in overall effect. Nor is Nozick's vision quite so draconian as it may first seem. His acceptance of the Lockean proviso (albeit in a weakened form) disallows acquisitions and voluntary transfers which would prevent others from concluding similar contracts. Where Rawls differs from Nozick is in his assertion that his (Rawls's) concept of justice applies not only to the special case where outcomes lead to monopolies, but also to the creation of surplus inequalities in general. For Rawls, justice demands that where there are surplus inequalities, these should be of greatest benefit to the most disadvantaged.

Justice and social policy

Clearly, which conceptual model of justice any government ultimately adopts has implications for social policy in that state. Within Nozick's model of a minimalist state, welfare is regarded as an unfair system designed to extort wealth from those who benefit from the inequalities which have arisen fairly from voluntary transactions. Nozick's minimalist state has no truck with interventions to redistribute wealth. Michaelman (1989) on the other hand, contends that a social minimum is implied by Rawls's theory of justice. In states where Rawls's account of justice prevails, welfare rights are regarded as legitimate, and as a necessary guarantee of basic liberty and equality of opportunity. Hence, the nub of Michaelman's argument is that welfare rights serve to fulfil certain critical needs which stand prior to (and are a condition of) basic liberty and opportunity.

For Ehman (1991: 313) however, neither Rawls nor Nozick offer a tenable definition of justice. Both accounts fail adequately to consider the need for well-being. Ehman contends that both accounts:

> rely upon the 'free market' to allocate resources ... and both require unanimity amongst the taxed in order to finance public goods. There is little attention in either to the *worth* of income or of liberty.

Ehman's argument is that neither income nor liberty is a sufficiently reliable index of well-being to serve as the defining principles of justice. What is wanted is a 'combination of utilitarian, perfectionist and need considerations'. Moreover, Ehman contends (p. 328) that Nozick's concept of justice does not 'proscribe taxation and subsidies', it proscribes *crime*. Nozick's account is about the rules of exchange, but these rules of transfer themselves go unevaluated. It may be that Nozick's account of formal justice is valid, but society needs more than justice in order to survive, it also needs compassion. For Nozick, compassion is not the business of the state, but of the individual. Nonetheless, Ehman (1991), in the tradition of Tawney (1964), argues for a conceptualisation of justice that goes beyond the 'mathematical' calculation of the effects of inequality, and insists on well-being as a necessary component.

Perhaps the key question at this point is what degree of inequality (even justly arrived-at inequality) can a society tolerate before it is no longer a society? Nozick's account (*pace* the Lockean proviso) allows for extreme inequalities, it even allows for a transaction which may severely harm one of the parties. Nozick (1974: 58) asserts that:

> Locke, of course, would hold that there are things others may not do to you by your permission; namely, those things you have no right to do to yourself. Locke would hold that your giving your permission cannot make it morally permissible for another to kill you, because you have no right to commit suicide. My non-paternalistic position holds that someone may choose (or permit another) to do to himself *anything*, unless he has acquired an obligation to some third party not to do or allow it.

For Rawls, the picture is far less clear. However, since privileges (inequalities) are vested in offices and positions, and exist within an overall system which benefits the least advantaged most, it is difficult to conceive how Rawls's theory could produce a circumstance in which self-harm is a just consequence.

What, then, would social policy principles look like if they were derived from these concepts of justice? Under Nozick, welfare would be the stuff of voluntary transactions between individuals. If I am ill I pay a doctor to find out what is wrong with me and give me medicine. I pay a teacher to teach me what I want to learn. I am free to choose any doctor or teacher who will enter into a transaction with me, at a price (or exchange of property) I can afford. If a social policy existed at all, its main thrust would be to protect such transactions against interference by the state. Indeed, I assume that I could set myself up as a teacher or a doctor and offer my services to others in the same way. Nozick may object that in fair voluntary transactions those who purchase my services will do so in the knowledge as to whether I command the pertinent skills. If I do not, sensible people will go elsewhere. However, Nozick is not in the business of protecting fools from themselves. Indeed, in theory, I could offer *any* services or goods I wished (even morally reprehensible ones), as long as these were obtained and supplied through voluntary (and not coercive) transactions. Nozick's concept of justice thus raises a number of moral questions.

By way of contrast, Rawls specifies that inequalities must be attached to offices to which all may aspire under conditions of fair equality of opportunity. In these circumstances, professions such as teacher and doctor may be regulated by the state. This affords some protection to the citizen, and the subsequent development of specialist skills benefits those who do not have them through the services provided by the proficient individual whilst occupying the office concerned. Where social policy is framed in accordance with Rawls's theory, resources will be allocated in a way that benefits most the least advantaged, and offices will be allocated on the basis of fair equality of opportunity. The concern is no longer simply to ensure the sanctity and voluntary nature of transactions, but to weigh them in terms of what inequalities are created, whom they benefit, and by how much. At face value this seems a more promising approach in terms both of the quality of life and social cohesion of any community. Certainly it must bear Nozick's criticism that this is a conceptualisation of justice that carries a whiff of state paternalism, but for 'paternalism' we could equally well read 'security'. Rawls's theory of justice does appear, at first sight, to lead to principles of social policy that respond to the intrinsic subject matter of such policy rather than external desiderata.

In sum, we are offered widely divergent conceptualisations of justice. First (other than for the preservation of fundamental rights such as the right not to be assaulted or killed), Nozick restricts the purview of justice to the processes, but not necessarily the outcomes, of human interactions. He argues for a minimal state which appears to rule out the development of social policies in the traditional sense of constituting a welfare state. Instead, welfare is a commodity, much like any other, to be bartered through personal voluntary transactions. Nozick's account allows help for the weak only in the form of *charity* (as an altruistic and voluntary transaction from richer to poorer deliberately in the favour of the poorer) but not as a right of the poor or an obligation or duty to be imposed on the rich.

For Rawls, justice must have regard not only to the processes of human interaction, but also to their outcomes. In this conceptualisation, the scope of liberty enjoyed by any one individual is limited by insistence that the same scope for freedom be available to others. For these boundaries to work, the privileges of inequality must, as I have said, attach to offices, not persons, and must be fairly gained according to the requirements of equality of opportunity.

In the end it comes down to preferences as to which concept of justice to employ in building, with others, the society in which one wishes to live. Nozick's concept will serve well the entrepreneurs, the risk-taking spirits, those who wish to live life in the fast lane where there are no limits as to how far one can rise, but also no limits as to how far one may fall. Supporters of Rawls, however, recognise that it is a part of the human condition that we have frailties as well as strengths, and that any kind of common welfare and security is bought at the price of forgoing some measure of individual liberty. Yet other writers may be attracted to Mill's utilitarian, social justice account, which has been developed in the modern context by Tawney (1964). Tawney recognised that personal advantages are seldom, if ever, gained without some dependence on, and assistance from, others in the society in which they arose, and that individuals therefore owe obligations to that society. Such duties are discharged by the sharing of resources and by some curtailment of individual liberty for the common good.

I will return to Nozick, Rawls and Walzer throughout the remainder of the book; however, it is important now to consider a key constituent of Rawls's justice: equality of opportunity. In what follows, I evaluate the efficacy of equality of opportunity as a mechanism, first, for ensuring equality of liberty and, second, for securing fairness in the distribution of inequalities.

Equality of opportunity

Notwithstanding the difficulties highlighted by MacIntyre, about the lack of any agreed basis for selecting one particular definition of justice over any other, we may recognise nevertheless that both Nozick and Rawls have referred to justice as defining the boundaries of individual liberty, and Walzer has acknowledged that there must be at least one kind of equality: that of universal social inclusion. Membership of a society is vital in order to participate in the negotiation of a working definition of justice for each salient sphere of human activity. One possible instrument for the discernment of such boundaries is equality of opportunity. For one person to have the possibility of exercising liberty to the same extent as every other, each must have the same potential opportunities open to them. If the scope of *potential* opportunities differs between people, then the quality of liberty must also differ between them. The outstanding question, therefore, with which we must deal in the remainder of the chapter, is what is meant by 'equality of opportunity'?

In the same way that the meaning of justice is contested, so too is the concept of 'equality of opportunity'. Baker (1987) sets out several approaches to defining the concept. The narrowest of these is meritocratic and industrial. Careers are open to all, and places are decided on merit alone. A broader definition (temporal and developmental) recognises that individuals have differing histories, and there is a need, therefore, to ensure equal chances as people develop and grow, prior to, as well as during, their careers. Baker offers a third model which includes fair chances of development and competition, but also provides affirmative action to compensate for previous disadvantages. An even more active concept would involve reverse discrimination (discrimination against a previously favoured group) to achieve proportionality. Blakemore and Drake (1996) take these and other models of equality of opportunity and interpret them within a spectrum of approaches ranging from minimalist to maximalist. In minimal accounts, equality of opportunity is simply concerned with securing fairness in the *procedures* used to fill offices and positions, to forbid direct discrimination and to disallow the use of irrelevant criteria in processes of selection. A maximal account, on the other hand, includes, but goes beyond, immediate decision-making to examine the broader context in which such events happen. Here we may include the equalisation of opportunities in education, training, environment, access, and so on. Eventually, the canvas may become so large as to encompass all aspects of society. Frankel (1983) recognised these points when he argued that two candidates may undergo a fair and identical test for a position, but apart from the test itself other factors may differ: one candidate may not have received an education appropriate to the sitting of the test, or may not have been encouraged or advised of the value of such an education, or may have been deprived of emotional support of a type which would foster such an understanding. Frankel is distinguishing here between, on the one hand, the removal of the immediate barriers (physical and otherwise) that prevent equality of opportunity, and, on the other hand, the positive actions required, perhaps over a lifetime, to make real any such amelioration of circumstances. We must bear in mind, therefore, how culture, development and time affect the securing of equality of opportunity. The point was reinforced by Tawney (1964: 74) in declaring that 'even in childhood, different strata of the population are distinguished by sharp contrasts of environment, of health, and of physical well-being'.

Notwithstanding the difficulties of implementing equal opportunity strategies, we can see at once the negative consequences that flow from a lack of equality. To begin with, any situation in which there is no equality of opportunity constitutes a contravention of Rawls's second principle. If inequalities belong to persons rather than to offices and positions, then privilege is distributed arbitrarily. Again, if inequalities are attached only to offices and positions, but some citizens are *unfairly* prevented from seeking such offices, then once more there is injustice in Rawls's sense of the word. We may see, then, that, 'equality of opportunity' does not set up any particular social arrangement as a desirable goal but merely requires the absence of artificial constraints on individual potential. Equality of opportunity is therefore a corollary of the liberty of the individual. Similarly, equality of opportunity is clearly an attack on privilege which we may define here as an advantage gained by means of force or discrimination. R. H. Tawney (1964: 57) agrees with Rawls when he (Tawney) writes that:

> to criticise inequality and to desire equality is not, as is sometimes suggested, to cherish the romantic illusion that men are equal in character and intelligence. It is to hold that, while their natural endowments differ profoundly, it is the mark of a civilized society to aim at eliminating such inequalities as have their source, not in individual differences, but in its own organisation, and that individual differences which are a source of social energy, are more likely to ripen and find expression if social inequalities are as far as practicable diminished.

Indeed, it is not only mainstream contemporary egalitarian thought, but also at least some of today's right-wing libertarian thinkers who would be quite content with this position. Libertarians attack political correctness; egalitarians attack sexism and racism. Each in their own way attempts to constrain and channel the thinking, organisation and practice of the other.

Equality of opportunity and the free market: congruent concepts?

The attributes of equality of opportunity, as I have just described them, have resonances with thinking usually associated with libertarians. One initially startling proposition is that there may be substantial similarities between egalitarian thought and Hayek's (1960) notion of the free market. If a market is free and remains free, rather than becoming rigged or dominated by a few powerful elites, then players within it would enjoy equality of opportunity. They would be able to make genuine choices, would be able freely to engage in transactions without coercion. These same ideas are found equally often in egalitarian writing. For example, Plant (1984: 9) asserts that:

> The egalitarian is only interested in restricting that range of choice which, if exercised, would enable an individual to impose on others a lower value on their freedom by devaluing the basic means which they have to pursue their ends.

Is not this a description of a desire to maintain a free market, one in which value or price is not imposed by a powerful few, but by the democratic exercise of choice by the many? How, in any truly free market, could there be an imposition of a lower value on the freedom of others? It may be, of course, that in real life the ideal of the free market is as unattainable as either absolute equality or absolute inequality. There is either a rigged market governed by cartels and monopolies, or there is a regulated market under the watchful eye of a monopolies and mergers commission and various other governmental regulators.

Barry (1965: 120) also recognises the affinity between equality of opportunity and the notion of a free market when he asserts that: 'to say that people should be equal is to say that their opportunities for satisfying whatever wants they may happen to have should be equal'. Frankel (1983) qualifies Barry's claim by arguing that such wants should only be satisfied insofar as they do not impinge upon the liberty of others. Accordingly, wants must be legitimate: the want to torture others is not legitimate for it impinges upon the liberty of the victim. Frankel therefore offers clear support for Rawls's first principle (concerning the extent of liberty).

But Frankel also argues that wants must be realistic. Though I may want to play the violin as superbly as Tasmin Little or Yehudi Menuhin, the desire is not, alas, realistic. Finally, Frankel introduces an interesting and controversial third constraint. A want should be affordable. Frankel's fundamental question is this: for any given example, is equality, or if you like, equality of opportunity, worth the cost? He reminds us that resources, time and energy are scarce in relation to wants, and, secondly, that wants are born of culture. Cultures differ, and therefore people's wants differ. To explore this point a little further, resources are scarce and some things cost more to achieve than others. For one particular person, it may cost a lot more to achieve a specific want than for another person to do so. To provide buses and trains for people who can climb up onto a platform costs less than providing buses and trains for people who can't. But both these groups have the same want: the use of public transport. Is society willing to meet the extra cost – in Frankel's terms, is the matter of sufficient importance – for access to be arranged for both groups, and for equality of opportunity to travel to prevail in this matter? The answer to this and similar questions will be reflected in the disability policies that a government introduces.

The costs of unequal opportunities

The counter argument, of course, is that there are costs associated with failing to provide equality of opportunity. Leaving aside questions of injustice, to award opportunities arbitrarily runs the risk of failing to maximise human potential. Such an action amounts, in fact, to the creation of a rigged market in opportunities, and rigged markets can be inefficient and costly not only for individuals, but also for commerce, for communities and for entire societies.

So when George Bernard Shaw (1913) asserted that we could 'not all write plays like he did' he was speaking the truth but missing the point. Equality of opportunity is not about everyone developing identical skills. It is instead about providing fair chances for each person to develop to his or her maximum potential such skills and capacities as he or she may command. In the absence of equal opportunities, in the lack of access to appropriate education, or in the unbreakable grip of discrimination, some potential author may never have had the opportunity to write plays. In the words of the poet Thomas Gray:

> Full many a flower is born to blush unseen,
> And waste its sweetness on the desert air.

Anti-egalitarians such as Green (1990) and Joseph and Sumption (1979) construe these points about equalising opportunities in education, access and employment as amounting to a desire for the lowest common denominator, as demands for the holding back of the ablest. Egalitarians contend, rather, that the inference to be drawn is the need to ensure a fair chance for all those who have, hitherto, been unfairly disadvantaged. As I have said, however, real-life decisions as to how to proceed are ultimately, of course, political ones.

Conclusions

The key task in this book lies not in finding the holy grail of the ultimate definition of justice, instead its purpose is more mundane: to develop a way of analysing social policies by measuring their outcomes against the stated principles of their creators. Whether the outcomes are desirable or not is for each of us to decide for ourselves. Likewise, we must each decide whether or not we agree with the particular concept of justice that underpins any set of policies. My aim here is provide tools so that the prevailing principles are rendered visible, the consequences of policy can be measured against stated principles, and we are thus in a position to decide our own attitudes towards particular policies.

The task set out at the beginning of the chapter was to discover some means of finding a point of balance between two undesirable situations: on the one hand, absolute equality (which implied a total lack of choice and, therefore, the absence of liberty) and, on the other hand, absolute and unconstrained liberty (resulting ultimately in extreme inequality). Writers on 'justice' have proposed various ways of achieving such points of balance. For example, one answer was suggested by Rawls who mooted a system within which the optimum conditions occurred where each person enjoyed basic liberties compatible with similar liberties for others. Furthermore, between absolute equality and absolute inequality there lay a point at which there existed inequalities, but these were *fair* inequalities. This point could be identified by the fact that the opportunities available to individuals to benefit from privileges were fair, and surplus inequalities were so arranged that greatest benefit accrued to those who were least advantaged.

However, as we saw, other authors, like Nozick, Walzer and Phillips, disagreed with Rawls. Nozick confined the definition of 'justice' to the processes of exchange, almost irrespective of outcome. These disagreements led MacIntyre to contend that there was, in fact, no certain way of deciding whose portrayal of justice was the 'right' one, and, indeed, that ultimately it depended on the point of view of the observer as to which model he or she preferred. For the purpose of this book we will see that in practice different governments have chosen to use different concepts of what is fair. While some have intervened to mitigate social inequalities, others have argued that it is for individuals to make their own way in the world as best they can. These latter governments have deregulated society, eschewed intervention, and have accepted (and even valued) widening inequalities.

The second half of the chapter concentrated on the 'how' as opposed to the 'what' of justice. For Nozick, justice could be achieved simply by letting people get on with living. There might be a need to preserve the peace and prevent fraud, but that would be about all. The Rawlsian approach to justice, however, enjoined the need to influence social outcomes as well as social processes. Rawls thus required a mechanism for intervention, namely, equality of opportunity. Here again, it soon became evident that this concept, too, was contested. Providing fair opportunities was not merely about fair tests, but about past and present conditions in people's lives. It was not enough that opportunities were open and fair in the here and now, it was also necessary to provide fair chances for the well-being and development of individuals to the utmost of their potential. In the next chapter I turn to the effects of, and responses to, injustice. These responses include the affirmation of rights, the recognition of needs, and the quest for empowerment.

5

Rights, Needs and Empowerment

Introduction

Three concepts – rights, needs and empowerment – stand at the heart of this chapter. The first task is to discuss the meaning of 'rights' and explore the relationship between rights and justice. Second, I introduce the concept of 'need' and consider the relationship between rights and needs. Finally, I conceive of 'empowerment' as a mechanism or process through which needs may be met and rights satisfied.

In the previous chapter it became clear that concepts of justice (and injustice) are essentially contested. For writers like Walzer (1983), Young (1990) and Phillips (1991, 1987), 'justice' is a social artifact. If these writers are correct, then it follows that different understandings of justice may prevail in different places under different sets of conditions. In this chapter our focus is on 'rights', and more specifically 'welfare rights'. Of particular concern is the relationship between rights and justice. Put simply, if definitions of rights are subordinate to definitions of justice, then as prevailing understandings of justice mutate, so too will the rights to which people are entitled. If, however, rights transcend justice, then people will enjoy certain rights notwithstanding local definitions of justice. Many commentators (Jones, 1994; Freeden, 1991; Feinberg, 1980) come to the conclusion that in reality both of these propositions can be true at the same time. They assert that there are different classes of rights. Some rights are based on moral and human imperatives and so stand superior to any local understanding of 'justice'. But other rights are derived from, and are therefore subject to, prevailing notions of 'justice' as embodied in specific legislation.

83

The second focus for the chapter is the concept of 'needs'. Traditional representations of 'need' emphasise the psychological and physical conditions necessary to sustain human life (Maslow, 1968, 1943) . Here, however, I draw on the work of Doyal and Gough (1990) who propose a fundamental set of social, as well as cognitive and physical, needs. More specifically, I contend that there is a relationship between 'rights' and 'needs' such that needs arise where rights are denied. The final key element of the chapter, 'empowerment' constitutes a process through which rights are acquired, recovered or realised with the result that social and physical needs are satisfied.

Rights

I have suggested that, like other social concepts, the notion of 'rights' is difficult to define. Freeden (1991: 2) explains the difficulty by reminding us that a social concept is shaped by 'the range of further concepts that are attached to and support it'. He also contends that each use of the word 'rights' will be 'plucked from a spectrum of possible meanings'. Of chief concern here, however, is the differentiation of unassailable rights from dependent rights. For Freeden dependent 'rights' gain their specific meanings in any particular setting according to the influence of adjacent concepts such as liberty, equality and justice. But Freeden (p. 7) draws a clear distinction between these dependent or contextual 'rights' and the (perhaps more profound) notion of a *human right* which he defines as:

> a conceptual device, expressed in linguistic form, that assigns priority to certain human or social attributes regarded as essential to the adequate functioning of a human being; that is intended to serve as a protective capsule for those attributes; and that appeals for deliberate action to ensure such protection.

Jones (1994) agrees that this class of rights is unassailable. He argues that human rights have three inherent qualities. First, they are imprescriptible, that is, they cannot be eroded by time. Second, they are inalienable, you can neither have them removed from you, nor can you relinquish them, even voluntarily. Third, they are indefeasible, they cannot be overridden or superseded. Indeed, Freeden (1991: 9) contends that the 'waiving of human rights is humanly destructive rather than logically impossible. Their absence would deprive a community of rational goals, indeed a means of survival'. We should note, then, that what both Freeden and Jones are saying is that human rights are of a different order than rights in general, for where human rights are denied, they do tangible harm not only to the individuals concerned, but also to the community in which the denial occurs. Where human rights are habitually and unendingly traduced, such a community cannot, ultimately, survive. Norman (1987: 136) concurs with this analysis. For him the concept 'marks out the most important and most valuable kinds of freedom which have a special protected status'. Human rights are in this sense *fundamental*. They constitute a special class of immutable rights, and they must, therefore, stand superior to any local or temporary conceptualisations of justice.

The more general use of the word 'rights' is of a different order than human rights. Here, any specific configuration of rights depends on prevailing conceptualisations of liberty, justice and equality of opportunity. In this sense, rights are both subordinate and dependent. Jones (1994) suggests that a great variety of these kinds of right are claimed or asserted. Claims may be expressed either positively or negatively, that is, either that we may act in a specific way, or that others may *not* act in a particular fashion towards us. So, for example, I may claim the positive right to vote in an election, but equally I may assert the right *not* to be physically assaulted by someone else. Two further points follow from the fact that these more general rights depend on the social and political contours of the state. First, that someone has laid claim to a right does not automatically mean that such a right is acknowledged in that state, and second, that the existence of a right is not the same thing as the honouring of a right. Rights have been (and no doubt will continue to be) either transgressed or refuted.

Where a right has been accepted and prevailing rules of justice are broken, then we may conclude that a right has been infringed or denied, and an injustice perpetrated. If a right is violated, a victim is entitled to compensation or redress. Again, it is not always the case that restitution occurs. Not all injustices are mended.

Origins of rights

To recap, scholars have differentiated between (unassailable) human rights and more general (dependent) rights. On what grounds have human rights been elevated to their superior position? Many scholars such as Frankel (1983) and Norman (1987) point to two sources as being the origins of rights. First, they argue that we acquire rights merely by dint of our belonging to a particular species of animal: *homo sapiens*. The fact that we are human beings, with the capacity to reason, accords us human rights. In passing, it might be said that this claim for uniqueness may not be so clear cut as it once seemed. There are two challenges, categorical and temporal. First, the category human is often distinguished from non-human by two qualities: ratiocination and consciousness of self. However, other animals such as gorillas and chimpanzees have demonstrated a level of language capacity and (though this remains a controversial claim) have also exhibited ratiocination and self-awareness (Savage-Rumbaugh *et al.*, 1998; Taylor-Parker and Gibson, 1990; Savage-Rumbaugh, 1986; Rumbaugh, 1977). The question arises, then, as to whether rights accorded to humans should also extend to animals. Secondly there is a temporal area of difficulty concerning the status of human embryos and foetuses. When does a human life begin? If, as some argue, human beings originate at conception, then abortion transgresses human rights. If, as others propose, human beings begin at birth, or at some other specified point during pregnancy, then before that specified point the embryo or foetus (according to this school of thought) does not constitute a human being and does not enjoy the protection of human rights, so that abortion amounts, in this analysis, to a further method of contraception. (For more detailed discussion of these issues see Kallianes and Rubenfeld, 1997; Berer, 1988; Himmelweit, 1988.) There are questions then, about who should be accorded, and at what point they should be accorded, human rights. These questions may challenge the unique underpinning of human rights.

More generally however, rights may take a number of forms. Hohfeld (1919) offers a legal analysis of rights which has stood the test of time. He proposes four categories of relationship between the possessor of a right, X, and another person, Y, and some object or action, A:

(1) X has a liberty or privilege to do A – when X has no duty towards Y not to do A, and Y has a 'no-right' towards X (that is, Y has no right to impede X from doing A).
(2) X claims A from Y – and Y has a duty towards X to do A.
(3) X has a power to bring about a consequence for Y.
(4) X has immunity – Y lacks a power to bring about a consequence for X.

These algebraic formulations may be expressed more plainly. There are, first of all, rights as liberties. These may include, for example, a right to freedom of worship, a right to free speech, and so forth. Next there are claims on others. Claims may be made as a result of contractual agreements or arise out of certain kinds of relationship. A claim may refer to an individual, an organisation or even a state. Thirdly there are powers, often associated with a particular status or office. There are, for example, those who have earned the right to certain honours, privileges or distinctions. Lastly, there are immunities, for example, the right not to be imprisoned unlawfully. Rights may thus entail differing forms of expression: liberties, claims, immunities and powers.

The function of rights

What is the function of rights? White (1984) offers several possibilities which may be brought under four general headings consistent with Hohfeld's analysis. These are benefits, choices, entitlements and sanctions. First, rights may confer benefits. It is a benefit, for example, to have the right not to be assaulted. Second, they may afford choices. The very notion of a right to vote involves choices in who should lead or govern a society. Third, rights may establish entitlements, our power to call on something or someone for support. If we have, under certain conditions, a right to money from the state, we are *ipso facto* entitled. Clearly, then, these kinds of rights are particularly relevant to social policy. Finally, rights may confer duties or powers of sanction. For example, we may have a right to deny something to someone. In Britain, a householder (except in the event of a legally obtained search warrant) has the right to deny entry to callers.

Many rights have been codified either into laws, into the accepted practice we call custom, or perhaps as a framework of moral values. Moral values are a particularly apt expression for the negative types of rights. For example, the ten commandments are *protections* as much as they are *adjurations*: with slight alteration, they may have been written, 'Thou shalt not steal *from me*'; 'Thou shalt not kill *me*'. By leaving out the words 'me' or 'my', the rights become generalised, and act not only as universal prohibitions, *'Thou shalt not steal'*, but also as universal immunities. We may see moral systems then, in this dual way: as being both protective and prohibitive at one and the same time.

But rights may be utilitarian or functional as well as moral or ethical in nature. Where rights apply equally to all members of a community, they preserve society and prevent conflict and disorder. The boundary that stands between the freedom of action of two persons' A and B, is that point at which either A's or B's rights are infringed by the other. At that point, the other party's freedom of action ends. The point marks the limit to one's autonomy. Go beyond it, and the other's rights are, as a result, contravened or suppressed. So when we come up against the other's rights, the result is some curtailment in the degree of autonomy we enjoy. The philosopher Immanual Kant (1786) studied this problem of autonomy. He suggested that at the limit of autonomy stood the boundary between the rights of different groups and individuals. For Kant, because human beings are capable of reason, they could understand that morality was in fact a system of codifying practical necessities. Moral laws were thus self-imposed, not externally enjoined upon us.

Beyond moral codes, the philosopher Roger Scruton (1982) discusses the idea of legal rights, and, in particular, the notion that legal rights may amount to the expression of a social contract. Scruton argues that the citizens of certain states have given up a degree of freedom (or in Kant's model, some degree of *autonomy*), in return for rights which have been clearly spelled out in the constitutions upon which such states were founded. Frequently a constitution guarantees benefits like equality before the law, the right to a fair trial and the right to seek compensation for some injustice. So there are legal rights enshrined in constitutions, or, in Britain, enunciated in Acts of Parliament and in case law. In this sense, a right is the embodiment of the prevailing conceptualisation of justice and acts as a safeguard for the prevailing conceptualisation of liberty.

It is to the prevailing notion of justice that people appeal on those difficult occasions when rights seem to be in conflict, one with another. For example, the playing of loud music may clash with a neighbour's right to peace and quiet. If no resolution is reached, then the law may be used to arbitrate and apply sanctions, protecting one householder's right, and confirming to the other that they don't have the right they thought they had. If there is no law, then a person may nominally have a right, but he or she could find that it is traduced by *force majeure*.

Rights to welfare

Since this book is concerned primarily with the principles of social policy, it is important to give scrutiny to a particular subset of rights: welfare rights. Does a right to welfare exist, and, if so, what are welfare rights and how may we conceive of them?

Writers such as Stoljar (1984) have produced cogent reasoning to argue that there is no 'right to welfare'. Briefly, Stoljar (pp. 105–7) proposes that a person A may suffer some accidental misfortune that prevents him or her from working and gaining the resources needed to live. But another person B, not being to blame for A's predicament, is, says Stoljar (p. 105), under no obligation to A morally or otherwise.

> Any human being ... has to make his [*sic*] own life according to his capacities and his wants. We are not all equal, nor do we want to end up with the same lives. What distinguishes our humanity is that we can and do accept personal differences and that we can grapple with them through moral argument. Yet even if it is false equality to make us all the same, there are differences that are humanly damaging and deeply affect our inter-individual relationships. A person, for example, can, through no fault of his own, suffer misfortune: illness, accident or economic loss, can seriously disable his possibilities of acting or working.

There are a number of responses that might be made to these kinds of argument. First, what is important is not the source of the impoverishment, but the locus of change. By this I mean that there may be an onus on society not only to train citizens for work but also to configure 'work' for citizens. Second, the introduction and maintenance of a system of mutual insurance may confer welfare rights on those who meet with the misfortunes that Stoljar describes. Third, other circumstances than those offered by Stoljar may give rise to welfare rights: for example, the right to welfare may arise as compensation for injustices stemming from inequality of opportunity. (We should note here Stoljar makes no reference to the possibility that 'disability from work' may arise as much from the contours of the working environment as from the incapacities of an individual.)

The main reason for raising Stoljar's argument is that it illustrates the point made towards the beginning of the chapter, that the notion of 'welfare rights' is essentially a contested one. For those who subscribe to Nozick's (1974) conceptualisation of justice, rights only come into play if transactions have been fraudulent. For those who agree with Rawls (1972), rights are more extensive in that they cover outcomes as well as processes. In this context, welfare rights constitute recognition of, and a response to, unfair inequalities stemming from social and political structures as much as from individual prejudice or fraudulent action. Here, welfare rights amount to a claim to redress, and from this perspective welfare rights are compensatory. They are a recognition that prevailing circumstances may favour some groups, but disadvantage others. In this context, one of the key assumptions underpinning the idea of welfare rights is that poverty is socially constructed (Lister, 1990; Novak, 1988; George and Wilding, 1984), being caused not by individual volition, but by differences in social status, educational opportunity, and access to work. Lister (1990: 40) in particular has argued that poverty impedes people's exercise of their rights:

> For poor people there can be a kind of negative feedback loop between their civil/legal and their social rights of citizenship ... restrictions on the exercise of legal citizenship rights in the sphere of the welfare state undermine poor people's rights of social citizenship.

Dahrendorf (1987) argues that a lack of welfare rights leads to a state of social exclusion today described by terms such as 'underclass' (Mann, 1994). He further contends that the existence of an underclass jeopardises the social contract itself. (If a group is excluded from defining social norms, why then should it comply with them?)

Clearly, then, governments may either accept or reject the claim that some specific welfare right exists. Governments may extend or constrain rights to benefits in the light of their view as to whether some particular disadvantage is attributable to personal or structural causes. We may see how welfare rights are, in this sense, subservient to prevailing beliefs about justice and equality.

Welfare rights are, then, a far more troublesome species within the genus of things we call 'rights'. It is not at all clear that welfare rights derive either from the fact of our humanity or from any code or constitution. What status should we give, for example, to the right to work, the right to a decent home, or the right to a living wage? The problem with these concepts is that they are not, inherently at least, legal rights, and there is dispute as to whether they constitute either moral rights or human rights or neither of these things.

In Britain, except under very special circumstances to do with race relations or sex discrimination, a person cannot start legal proceedings simply because he or she has been refused an interview for a job, or cannot afford to buy or rent a home. Whom do you prosecute because you have no work? Which employer is it that is denying you your 'right'? Do you prosecute the state for your unemployment, arguing that its economic and industrial policies are to blame? If so, under which law do you press your action? If these are not legal rights, what then are they?

Can welfare rights be thought of as claims based on moral precepts? In the chapter on freedom and equality I referred to the fact that many political philosophers from Plato onwards suggested the existence of a social contract between a state and its individual citizens. In return for the protection of the state, citizens give up a certain amount of autonomy. Let us consider, therefore, a situation in which, in order to operate at maximum industrial efficiency, the state must have a certain amount of surplus labour which remains for some or all of the time, unemployed. Has the state in these circumstances a moral obligation to sustain and support those who make the sacrifice of not working? Have they, in turn, a 'right' – a moral claim – to such support?

Or, again, take an example where the state has accepted an obligation so to configure itself and its institutions that it serves fairly all its citizens in the conduct of social life. Nobody is to be excluded. Have those whom it fails to serve a moral entitlement or claim to compensation? Certainly, arguments like these have been made in respect of disabled people in Britain (Drake, 1999; Barnes and Oliver, 1998).

I have said that the reason that all these questions cause so much dissension is that there is no general accord that this class of concepts should be counted amongst those things that constitute rights, nor is there any consensus about the responsibilities and obligations of the state. Karl Popper (1945) has argued that social laws are conditional, not causal, and as a result generalisations about society have different degrees of probability. No generalisations are necessarily true. Nor yet is there agreement about the causes of inequality. Dahrendorf (1975, 1969) explains inequality as arising from several factors, such as social stratification, the division of labour, the distribution of power and the mechanism by which social norms are created so that they reflect the interests of the powerful.

It is on this expansive field of uncertainty that the most furious battles are being fought. To highlight how disputable these kinds of 'rights' are, it is entirely possible (using a concept of justice restricted to processes rather than to outcomes) to build an argument against the examples of 'rights' I gave earlier in the chapter concerning a state's obligations towards unemployed or disabled people.

First, it may be argued that, if people are unemployed, this may be due not to cyclical trading conditions or inbuilt reserves of surplus labour in the economy, but rather to the individual failure of each unemployed person to secure work, either by a refusal to look for it, by a refusal to train for it, or by their failing to accept the jobs on offer. Given that work is advertised daily in job centres and news-papers, the state has no moral obligation towards unemployed people.

Second, owners of buildings have the liberty to commission what facilities they will, and employers may employ whomsoever they wish. If disabled people are thus excluded, they must adapt them-selves to prevailing circumstances, purchase such equipment as will help them negotiate buildings, and train to acquire the skills that are attractive to employers. Since the state already meets a moral claim, first, by asking employers to make reasonable accommodations for disabled employees, and, second, by providing health and social ser-vice facilities and social security benefits, it has no additional obliga-tion, and certainly has no right to curtail any further the liberties of employers. Inequality is a state of nature. That some have benefited and others have lost is only to be expected. The state has no favourites, and it owes no favours. It is not for the state to compensate the unfortunate, its sole business is the preservation of law and order.

Let me be clear that the arguments I have just rehearsed in the pre-vious two paragraphs do not represent my own views. I offer them merely as examples to show that the way in which we perceive the role of the state influences directly our perception of, and our atti-tudes towards, those types of 'rights' which are classed as moral claims rather than legal entitlements.

The politics of rights

Attitudes towards 'rights' are ultimately political. Those on the far right of the political spectrum are more sympathetic to Nozick's (1974) view that justice is a concept to be applied only to mecha-nisms, as opposed to outcomes. That inequalities arise is undisputed, but inasmuch as these inequalities stem from fairly agreed and exe-cuted exchanges, they are not unjust inequalities, and the worst off thus have no further claim on the better off. In a democracy which operates a free market there can be no 'rights' to welfare. The con-comitant argument here is that state-run welfare and social security programmes must not be used as a mechanism for the redistribution of wealth, for to do so would be to infringe the liberty of those individuals who must give up some of their means and resources.

In accordance with this view, Joseph and Sumption (1979) declared that they wrote their book, 'to challenge the belief that it is a proper function of the state to influence the distribution of wealth for its own sake'. The wealthy have earned their money, it is wrong to pilfer it and give it to the idle and the feckless. Scruton (1984, 1982) therefore characterises social security not as the fulfilment of a state responsibility, but as the provision of charity, since 'it is the function of charity to provide for the poor'.

There is, then, a profound and deep-rooted political argument here about the status of welfare. For the political right, social security amounts to charity given at the prompting of human emotions such as pity and compassion. There are no such things as welfare rights. Individuals have no claims upon the state beyond the extent of their National Insurance contributions. The state has not been responsible for the plight of welfare claimants, their deprivation is not systemic. They are individually responsible for their own circumstances, their claims, morally and in all other ways, are invalid.

For the radical left, however, justice must be concerned with outcome as much as with process, and, far from being a gift, social security is a right, since all contribute to it when they are in work. Moreover, in the absence of equality of opportunity, the foundation of the wealth (particularly inherited wealth) enjoyed by the rich is not legitimate. Redistribution is, therefore, a justified purpose and social security is a proper mechanism for the achievement of such redistribution (Novak, 1988; Foot and Evans, 1982, 1977; Socialist Party of Great Britain, 1948). Drabble (1988) argued that it constituted an injustice where inequality was exacerbated by the use of high unemployment as a means of dealing with inflation. In such situations, contrary to the ideal of a free market, choice was restricted to those with high skills and deep purses.

In summary, the left asserts that social security is a right based on two claims: the actuality of prior contributions and a moral claim stemming from unjust inequalities. The right argues that social security is charity born of human goodness, but rights are not involved here. There are no valid claims to be made either on the wealthy or on the state. The state, like the free market, causes neither inequality nor injustice.

Are there other arguments that might support the idea of 'welfare rights' beyond the purely political? Jones (1994) suggests three reasons why we might treat welfare rights as bona fide rights. First, welfare is fundamental to quality of (and in some circumstances, the sustaining of) life itself. It bears, in this respect, close resemblance to human rights. Second, welfare is an investment in society, not just in individuals. To repair an elderly lady's house is also to upgrade the national housing stock. Third, a right to welfare obviates the stigma of charity which demeans the human condition.

Justice and rights

Before leaving the subject of rights there is one more matter for us to consider. Earlier in the chapter unassailable human rights were contrasted with dependent rights. It was suggested that dependent rights varied according to the specific conceptualisation of justice at play in a particular society. The point to be made here is this. What manner of right is it for an individual to participate in the construction of the meaning of justice to which his or her dependent rights are subject?

Almost all the writers whose work we have considered agree that the right to participate in the defining of justice is an unassailable and fundamental right of citizenship. To exclude some individuals from the fashioning of such an important social construct is to create different categories or levels of human beings and thus compromise basic human rights. So Kymlicka (1990: 4) writes:

> if a theory claimed that some people were not entitled to equal consideration from the government, if it claimed that certain kinds of people just do not matter as much as others, then most people in the modern world would reject that theory immediately.

This view concurs with – indeed, draws on – Dworkin's (1977) suggestion that the idea that each person matters equally is 'at the heart of all plausible political theories'. Definitions of justice and of dependent rights are only justly reached when the people subject to such definitions have enjoyed an equal and inclusive part in their creation. Where some are excluded from the process of definition, it follows that certain rights have been traduced.

In reality, however, it is hard to imagine that all citizens can take an equal and inclusive part in creating the basic parameters of justice, liberty, equality and other critical social concepts. Power is distributed differentially through societies (Lukes, 1974; Gramsci, 1971). In any particular population, those who are powerful may exercise considerable influence over definitions of justice, injustice and rights. But weaker members and groups may find it much harder to get their voices heard. To participate more effectively, they would need to achieve 'empowerment', but prevailing definitions of justice, injustice and rights may actually load the dice against them in their quest for that empowerment (Gaventa, 1980; Crenson, 1971).

Though they clash on what constitutes justice (and, therefore, on what amounts to injustice) Nozick (1974), Rawls (1972) and Walzer (1983) all agree that, where injustices arise, there is an obligation on authority to rectify the unjust situation. This may involve the overturning of some particular set of circumstances or entail the provision of restitution or compensation. Indeed, one role for social policy may be to provide redress as a response to unjust inequalities. In this sense, social policy constitutes an attempt by the state to fulfil its obligations to, and maintain the welfare rights of, its citizens. In this way, rights can be seen as a sort of qualitative measuring device, a way of evaluating the relationship between the state and the individual.

However, since people hold different views about what constitutes justice and injustice, they will disagree about the fairness of the impacts of social policies. Those who see justice as applying to outcomes will look for social policies which support welfare rights. Those who regard justice as restricted to the fairness of acquisitions and transfers will regard redistributive or restrictive policies as unjust. Clearly, then, depending on the prevailing policy principles and the point of view of the observer, some may believe that far from remedying injustice new injustices are being created through the very purposes, contours and implementation of social policies themselves. In other words, the claim would be that an unjust definition of justice was being used to guide policy, and that the rights being acknowledged by such policies were not, in fact, rights at all. We may see, therefore, why it is that concepts like 'welfare rights' and 'the right to work' attract such inflamed debate.

One consequence of the denial of rights is the creation of 'needs'. Here, we may see 'needs' as arising from disadvantages or material deficits caused by injustice. Needs will only be fully remedied if action follows to overturn the infringement or denial of rights suffered by the victims. It is to 'needs', therefore, that we now turn.

Needs and empowerment

Doyal and Gough (1990) argue that there is a direct link between impaired social participation and the concept of serious harm. For

them (pp. 79, 81), the satisfaction of basic welfare needs is critical to
the avoidance of fundamental impairments, social as well as physiological:

> Since the protection of the health of individuals, their learning and the
> growth of their emotional maturity are themselves social processes, they
> necessarily entail individuals interacting in social groups ... in all cultures it
> is necessary somehow to create food, shelter and other [need] satisfiers [*sic*]
> for what are defined as 'normal' levels of health to be achieved collectively.

For Doyal and Gough, unmet need is a social artifact. Basic needs
can only be met through social inclusion. Social exclusion results in
the absence (to a lesser or greater extent) of basic welfare needs such
as nutrition, health, education and shelter. There are, therefore, societal preconditions (of inclusion) for the satisfaction of these basic
needs (Doyal and Gough, 1991, chapter 5). However, it is possible to
extrapolate the consequences of social exclusion to point to other,
less immanent but equally important needs normally thought to constitute citizenship (see Harris, 1987, chapters 3 to 5).

Doyal and Gough, then, argue that needs are a consequence of
social exclusion, and I argue that social exclusion both results in, and
stems from, a denial of rights and especially a denial of participation
in the definition of those rights that stand subordinate to definitions
of justice. Accordingly, it is possible to define 'needs' as the specific
disadvantage that occurs when rights are traduced. In particular, it is
the redress necessary to offset unjust inequalities. Hitherto, particularly in the applied social sciences, needs have been thought of as
being individual attributes ('He needs physiotherapy', 'She needs
debt counselling'). In the context of the current discussion, however,
needs are satisfied as much by interventions in the broader environment as by the making of changes in the circumstances of individuals. For example, the need may be for investment and jobs in an area,
not just new skills for an unemployed person. There may be a need
for new architectural standards of access as much as for a new
wheelchair design for disabled persons.

Earlier in the chapter I argued that power was distributed differentially through societies (Lukes, 1974; Gramsci, 1971) and powerful
people could exercise considerable influence over definitions of
justice, injustice and rights. The weak could find it difficult to be
heard. Empowerment was needed if participation was to be real and
effective, However, prevailing definitions of justice and rights might

hinder or preclude social inclusion (Gaventa, 1980; Crenson, 1971). For this reason writers like Beresford and Croft (1993) and Lister (1990) insist that a process of empowerment prefigures some shift in the structure and distribution of power. The conceptualisation of justice which supported a disempowering and exclusive society would need to be amended, or even replaced, by a competing and more plural conceptualisation of justice. Speaking more broadly, we may expect to find certain affinities between particular concepts of justice and other kinds of policy principles. So, for example, Rawls's concept of justice, concerned as it is with outcomes (and particularly with the distribution of inequalities), would sit happily with the plural policy principles I described in Chapter 2. These not only promote difference, encourage diversity and allow for change, but also support equality of opportunity through support for constitutive policy aims. However, concepts of justice not concerned with outcomes may more easily underpin social policies founded on particularistic principles. Inasmuch as process-based (Nozickean) definitions of justice allow for arbitrary and unequal outcomes, the interests and privileges of dominant groups will be left intact.

What emerges from this analysis is that in order for needs to be fulfilled, it is not sufficient to intervene only to effect change in individuals. It is also necessary to alter environments, and, in particular, some redistribution of power is required so that disadvantaged groups or communities become empowered. Empowerment is not, therefore, a process in which a more powerful group effects emendations in the conditions of another (for example, social workers seeking to 'modify' the behaviours or circumstances of their clients). On the contrary, writers such as Oliver (1990) and Beresford and Croft (1993, 1989, 1984) contend that empowerment can only be achieved by disadvantaged individuals or groups for themselves, that it cannot be a gift transferred from one to another. Power-holders may relinquish some of their power, but subordinate groups must acquire and exercise power themselves. Within the context of my analysis in this book, one route to empowerment would be to challenge prevailing definitions of justice and rights. This would, of course, amount to challenging prevailing norms and values. The aim would be to bring about policies and practices based on new principles which recognised diversity, difference and the need for change. Such radical change has been attempted at many points in history. Some have chosen the path of revolution, others have sought to employ democratic methods such as election to those offices and positions in which reside the authority to effect change. We can see, then, why egalitarians set such enormous store by equality of opportunity as a mechanism for the allocation of offices and positions in society. In British history, certain categories of people have faced discrimination and have been excluded from key offices.

To give just one example, disabled people have, until very recently, been substantially absent from positions of political authority, and have been almost invisible in the social and political landscape. One consequence of that absence has been the silence of legislation on the matter of discrimination against them. It is only very recently, and as the result of the emergence of a strong disability movement, that governments have begun to give serious attention to the need for effective anti-discrimination legislation (Drake, 1999; Barnes, 1991; Pagel, 1988).

Conclusion

This chapter has been concerned with the concepts of rights, needs and empowerment. I have argued that, for any particular society, the identification of rights is inextricably linked with prevailing definitions of justice. Rights become tangible in conditions of injustice, which circumstances may include instances of unfair inequality. As to 'welfare rights', some thinkers such as Scruton (1984, 1982) or Stoljar (1984) argue that welfare is not a question of rights but one of charity; but others, such as Twine (1994), Jones (1994) and Marshall (1992), argue that welfare rights exist, first because welfare has been purchased through insurance, and second because in circumstances of unfair inequalities, where equality of opportunity is absent, welfare rights represent the redress due if justice (as contract) is to be restored. The reader will see that policy principles which promote the interests of some groups of the population over others are likely to create inequalities involving privilege for some and disadvantage for others. Insofar as unjust inequalities are created, rights to welfare provide a mechanism of redress or compensation. But more than this, they also indicate the existence of needs as the tangible expression of the disadvantages thus created, and they foreshadow the necessity of empowerment in order to bring about change and the fulfilment of rights.

Social policies may be monolithic and unilateral, but they may also be constructed in ways which accommodate diversity and difference.

The next chapter discusses the qualities that must be found in social policies, the principles on which they must stand, if they are to facilitate diversity within a population and allow for social change. Thereafter, in Chapter 7 I bring together all the concepts discussed in the book so far – justice, liberty, equality, rights and diversity – in order to illuminate the concept of 'citizenship'.

6

Diversity, Difference and Change

If societies were uniform and unchanging, if their members shared identical values, beliefs and ambitions, if they possessed a common culture and abided by universally agreed rules, then we may imagine that the formulation of policy and implementation of practice would be straightforward and unproblematic. Given such circumstances there could be little need for a book like this. In reality, however, values, principles and policies are unendingly challenged and policy outcomes discriminate between groups in a variety of ways (Mishra, 1981). Because societies, governments and political structures change over time, so too do the values, principles and policies that hold sway (Colebatch, 1998; Vincent, 1992, 1987). Nor are societies homogeneous; they are plural entities which contain sub-groups that differ from each other, culturally, socially and politically (Giddens, 1995; Waters, 1994; Seidman and Wagner, 1992; Craib, 1992). Clearly, then, for a society to continue to remain viable through time, a government must – to whatever degree – take into account the diverse values and interests of distinct caucuses within a population. This chapter is about the potential difficulties involved in policy-making for plural societies. The recognition of diversity is a first step, but then a state must set about evolving principles and policies able to accommodate socially and culturally distinct groups. Responses to diversity are important since the acknowledgement of basic differences and the degree of respect for competing values will determine the quality of citizenship.

The chapter begins with an analysis of some key elements that have contributed to the emergence of diversity in the modern world. These include the mobility of populations and the structuring of institutions such as family and work. Next, I explore interpretations of diversity and consider the potential range of state responses to it. There are many possible strategies for policy creation in heterogeneous societies. These range from imposed uniformity to negotiated plurality. Imposed uniformity is a totalitarian approach. Its aim is to stamp out difference, either by melding groups together and synthesising their values into one overall ideology, or by ignoring or eradicating some values (and in the worst cases, even some groups) completely, so that others may prevail unchallenged. At the other end of the spectrum, a more subtle and complex strategy involves attempts to achieve consensus and the acceptance of plurality. In this approach diverse values are afforded equal respect (Blakemore and Drake, 1996). Of course, for a society to survive intact there are limits as to how greatly values can vary without coming into conflict one with another. At the extreme, a clash of values could be so violent as to cause the fragmentation of the state (Calvert, 1983; Cohan, 1975; Lipset, 1969; see also Lee and Raban, 1988 on social policy). As a third coping strategy, a state may adopt a mixed or selective approach to diversity, seeking to maintain traditional or preferred values, but giving some acknowledgement to *certain* values of other, less powerful or less dominant groups in society. Finally, a fourth strategy may be to compartmentalise, that is, to devolve power. Here, although the main state entity continues, there is some measure of devolution (Bogdanor, 1999, 1979; Mackintosh, 1968). A degree of autonomy is granted in specific areas of concern so that differing values may prevail in separate social domains, allowing diversity to persist and, perhaps, flourish.

The focus on social policy is maintained in the third main part of the chapter which considers the management of change. I argue that where inflexible (or even totalitarian) principles dominate, change may be more difficult to achieve since it involves some alteration to prevailing values and can, therefore, be a threat. I conclude that even though change is natural to the human condition, the management of diversity and the introduction of change require (and are best achieved by) policy principles able to accommodate a variety of customs, traditions and ways of life.

The chapter closes with the argument that a state's approach to a diverse population and the policies derived from that approach are crucial in defining the experience of citizenship enjoyed by each community. Each of the strategies I describe in the chapter will yield different kinds of outcomes for citizens, according to their own specific circumstances, the existing policy montage, and the values and aims of the prevailing government.

Key factors in the creation of diversity

Many factors contribute to the emergence of diversified cultures and societies. Here I consider just three of the most important elements: population mobility (as exemplified by migration), changing family structures (as evinced in the shift from traditional, somewhat uniform, arrangements to more fragmented patterns of family life), and, finally, changes in labour market participation (as witnessed by the increasing role of women in the world of work).

Migration

Perhaps one of the most important contributions to social diversity has been the growing mobility of populations. The twentieth century has seen increasing flows of labour, not only within states but across national boundaries. This mobility was accelerated by colonisation, by disasters such as war and famine, and by demand for workers in industrialised nations. The United States, for example, received 15 million immigrants between 1945 and 1985 (Peach *et al.*, 1988). There has also been a widening 'wealth' gap between rich and poor nations, as well as between rich and poor groups and individuals within nations (Marquand, 1997). The resulting political and economic migration has fostered greater ethnic, social and cultural diversity.

Even so, it would be wrong to overestimate the impact of physical migration. For example, it is true that since 1945 Britain has seen an inflow of labour from the West Indies, Africa, Asia, the Antipodes, Eastern Europe and the Far East (Peach *et al.*, 1988). Nevertheless, white people still account for 94.5 per cent of the population (Office of Population Censuses and Surveys, 1993). The next largest ethnic group in Britain is those of Indian origin, but they constitute only 1.5 per cent of the total population (Office of Population Censuses and Surveys, 1993). If we look beyond the physical movement of peoples, however, we may observe the effects of culturally integrative (or invasive) forces such as global commerce, the mass media and the internet (Giddens, 1999; Olds, 1999; Kiely and Marfleet, 1998; Panikkar, 1995; Dunning, 1993; Grant, 1992).

Family structure

Diversity has also been reflected in major changes to traditional social arrangements, most notably in the structure of the family. For example, in the twentieth century Britain saw a sustained trend away from extended families towards smaller, nuclear families. More recently still, the institution of marriage has become just one of a variety of forms of partnership. As a further token of this fragmentation, lone parenthood has increased from 7 per cent of all families in 1971 to 22 per cent in 1998/9. During the same period married or cohabiting couples decreased from 92 per cent to 75 per cent of all families (Office for National Statistics, 2000). These data mirror a diminution in the average size of households from 4.6 persons in 1901 to 2.6 in 1985 (Halsey, 1988). In accordance with this trend towards a more atomised society, there has been a large increase in the proportion of people living alone, from 4 per cent of households in 1961 to 14 per cent by 1998/9 (Office for National Statistics, 2000). There has also been a corresponding increase in divorces, from 25,000 in 1961 to 145,000 in 1998 (Office for National Statistics, 2000). Taken together, these figures draw our attention to a splintering of social patterns and arrangements, a greater diversity of lifestyles and a clearer emphasis on individual autonomy.

Labour market participation

Further diversity has emerged in other key institutions such as the world of work. One of the most visible trends of the twentieth century was the increasing role of women in work and especially their participation in part-time work. Halsey (1988) has noted the particular advance of married women entering into employment. In 1931 just 10 per cent of married women had jobs. By 1985 the proportion was 52 per cent. A second major phenomenon has been the sharpening of a division between the employed and the excluded. Much academic argument has been devoted to the notion of an 'underclass', a concept intended to demarcate a group alienated from mainstream (work-based) cultures and norms (MacDonald, 1997; Mingione, 1996; Murray, 1996, 1994; Mann, 1994; Morris, 1994; Smith, 1992; Brown, 1990). In particular, Halsey (1988) highlights the increasing numbers of economically inactive men. We may also note the changes in work itself, with the retreat of agriculture and manufacturing and a corresponding growth in high technology occupations and service industries (Giddens, 1999; Marquand, 1997; Burrows and Loader, 1994). All of these factors account for the development of economies and workforces very different from those that existed even fifty years ago.

I have used several examples to propose increased diversity in major facets of contemporary society, in the mobility of populations, in their social and domestic arrangements, and in their working (or non-working) lives. I now turn to consider the spectrum of various responses that a state may adopt where there exists a broad range of values within a heterogeneous society.

Meanings of diversity and difference

Beyond changes in the make-up of populations and patterns of social life, the terms *diversity* and *difference* carry deeper connotations. To understand these it is important to know that the terms come from particular contexts, specifically from the fields of feminism and anti-racism (Hallett, 1996; Young, 1990) and, second, that they are most often used to counter the view that societies are homogeneous and based on universal rules. Young (1990: 7), for example, argues for a 'positive sense of difference' and urges a 'politics that attends to rather than represses difference'. The argument here, put forward *inter alia* by Young (1990), Lister (1997), Frazer and Lacey (1993), and Phillips (1998, 1991, 1987), is that individuals and groups differ from each other in significant ways, racially, culturally and by their gender. The term *diversity* is used to acknowledge the existence of these differences, but, more than this, it is used tacitly to convey the value statement or proposition that such differences should be regarded positively and should be encouraged. Consequently, political, social, and economic principles and policies should accommodate these differences so that people have their particular values and cultural needs respected. At the same time however, *diversity* is also used to signify that certain commonalities should be observed. In particular, notwithstanding any specific differences, people should be entitled to equal treatment as citizens. Clearly then, *diversity* and *difference* are difficult terms to use with any precision because they are complex and carry referential and contextual, as well as concrete meanings. As Hallett (1996: 9) tells us, they are often used within postmodern theories to contrast the local and specific with the uniform and universal. The key postmodern argument is that grand ideologies such as liberalism, Marxism, capitalism or patriarchy are in decline. The political landscape is becoming more variegated and devolved (Williams, 1992).

Burrows and Loader (1994) agree. They argue that the direction of social and economic change in Western societies has been away from the large-scale and uniform and towards the fragmented and diverse. Briefly (and perhaps to oversimplify the matter), the post-war world saw industry, commerce and the production of consumer goods carried out along the conveyor belts of mass production enterprises. Monolithic economies, routinised production methods, and heavily regimented work were matched by equally inflexible systems of welfare. These ideas have been bound together in a social and economic analysis given the overall title 'Fordism' (Burrows *et al.*, 1992; Hall, 1989). The argument now is that these large-scale industrial structures and the quotidian order they brought to the lives of wage-earning populations are giving way to new, much more splintered patterns of work. Heavy, mechanical, production-line industries have become far less prominent as new forms of work have developed, particularly in the service sector, in retail services and through the rapid expansion of information technology. Accordingly, some writers (Burrows and Loader, 1994; Burrows *et al.*, 1992) argue that we are approaching, or have arrived at, a 'post-Fordist' era, the hallmarks of which are flexibility and fragmentation. Hall (1989) contends that the product differentiation that has happened in the world of work is reflected in society at large. There has been a multiplication of social worlds, greater acknowledgement of cultural and ethnic diversity and a divergence in the mundane forms of family life. Charles (2000) examines the pressures that these new social worlds produce. Her extensive review of new social movements leads her to propose (after Melucci, 1989) that contemporary European social movements differ from those of the past by focusing not on class conflict within a given (capitalist nation state) context but on systemic change. Charles (2000: 31), drawing on the work of Habermas (1981) and Touraine (1981, 1977), concludes that the aims of new social movements are:

> primarily cultural rather than political, bringing about social change through the transformation of cultural codes and collective identities. They are concerned with cultural reproduction, social integration and socialisation and seek to defend the life world from encroachment by the system.

As a result of this state of social, economic and political flux, Burrows *et al.* (1992) contend that where cultures, societies, and political structures subscribe to a greater variety of values and norms, people conduct much more varied kinds of lives, and are not as willing to subordinate themselves to routine. Extensive social change of this kind has consequences for states, for social policy and for welfare more generally. Kriesi *et al.* (1995) argue that social change can operate at a number of levels. First, change can affect not only the identities of state organisations, but also their political structures and public attitudes towards them. Kriesi *et al.* elaborate four kinds of impact that social movements may have on political systems: sensitising; procedural; substantive; and structural. Charles (2000: 64) clarifies each of these categories. She explains that 'sensitising' impacts are those which bring new issues onto the political agenda and so influence public attitudes. Procedural impacts relate to the gaining of access to political systems and to subsequent acceptance as politically legitimate. Substantive impacts refer to the achievement of tangible and real policy objectives by social movements.Structural impacts involve changes in political opportunities and patterns of alliance, authority or representation. We may see, then, that the dialectical effects of new social movements on the existing political landscape can promote difference and diversity in government, in policy formulation and in day-to-day implementation and practice. What may this momentum for change mean for welfare?

The recognition of difference and promotion of diversity have affected welfare policy and practice in at least three key ways. First, post-war welfare in Britain was a largely monolithic and state-led phenomenon, but in recent years a more mixed economy of welfare has come into being (Newman and Clarke, 1994; Langan and Clarke, 1994; Wistow *et al.*, 1994; Farnham and Horton, 1992; McCarthy, 1989). Indeed, both Labour and Conservatives have been eager to curtail the state supply of welfare, notwithstanding the economic growth and robust commercial conditions of the 1990s. Second, functional divisions (some now being reversed by a New Labour government) were introduced into social administration: for example a split between purchasers of service and those who provide them, with new relationships to be based on contractual agreements (Anderson, 1990; Gutch, 1989; Kunz *et al.*, 1989). Third, some renegotiation of power structures and greater awareness of equal opportunity issues have led to a greater emphasis on user consultation and participation (Pithouse and Williamson, 1997; Drake, 1992; Croft and Beresford, 1989; Barker and Peck, 1987).

The policy montage in Britain is beginning to reflect the diversity of the communities that make up the total population, but there is still a long way to go. A recent major trend has been for a 'managing diversity' approach in the world of work (Kandola *et al.*, 1995; O'Neilly, 1995; Behrens, 1993; Behrens and Auluck, 1993). These writers argue that in seeking to promote anti-discriminatory policies and practices, the focus has been on individual factors such as religion, race, gender, age and disability. These social divisions were frequently used to highlight differences between some particular cluster of citizens and, as it were, the rest of 'mainstream' society. For the most part, differences tend to underscore some special attribute of the cluster in question, and give rise to the expectation of (or posit a requirement for) special treatment or redress. However, a 'managing diversity' approach focuses instead much more on environmental barriers and the benefits to be gained from eclectic communities and workforces.

From this perspective we see the potential advantages for employers of diverse and multi-skilled workforces, and for communities of wide-ranging sources of knowledge and wisdom. At the same time, we see more clearly the disadvantages that accrue where policies subscribe to – and reinforce – discriminatory values and result in either inadvertent or deliberate discrimination against members of subordinate and less powerful groups. Indeed, policies may allow discrimination and disadvantage *by default*. Though governments may not cause some particular discrimination themselves, they may, by *failing* to institute certain policies, allow specific groups to be treated detrimentally. This crucial point is highlighted in the following examples drawn from contemporary British society regarding discrimination in matters of gender, ethnicity, age and disability.

Gender

It has been a tenacious twentieth-century value that men work and women raise families. Such a division stood at the heart of the Beveridge Report (1942) which assumed explicitly that married women would not require social security since they could depend on their husbands' resources. Only relatively recently have governments begun to equalise the state's treatment of men and women workers.

However, in the world of work the residue of a patriarchal ideology remains strong and 'glass ceilings' (unobserved but real discriminatory structures, attitudes and practices) abound in many professions such that few (or even no) women are found in the highest positions in the top professions (Charles, 2000; Blakemore and Drake, 1996). More generally, Glendinning and Miller (1987) claim that there has been a 'feminisation of poverty'. For Rolfe (1999), disadvantages are both structural and chronic. From school onwards there is evident job segregation between men and women. Careers' services have signally failed to tackle gender stereotyping. For example, women constitute 97 per cent of the applicants for training as hairdressers and childminders whereas men make up 99 per cent of those going into the electrical, plumbing and construction trades. Rolfe's argument that gender segregation is 'pronounced all the way up the academic ladder' is supported by Bassnett (1999: 2), who points to the 'minute percentage of women professors, the even smaller percentage of senior women in administration, [and] the minuscule number of women vice-chancellors'. Clare (1999) reports that, across the board, male graduates tend to earn about 20 per cent more than female graduates. The average wage of men who were employed after graduating in 1998 was £14,619. The average salary for women who graduated in 1998 was £2,318 lower at just £12,301. Beyond the academic world, the picture is pretty much the same. Davis (1996) reveals that in 1990, 80 out of 90 directors of social services were men. The imbalance is also apparent in politics. Of the 659 MPs elected in the general election of 1997, only 120 (18 per cent) were women. Even this figure represents an enormous advance on the number in the previous Parliament, a mere 63 (Landale and Bowditch, 1997).

The inferior position occupied by women is replicated across all key areas of economic and industrial life. In education, males tend to predominate in those areas of study that lead to the better paid careers (Equal Opportunities Commission, 1998a,b,c,d). Far more men than women take 'A' levels in mathematics, the physical sciences, computing and technology, whereas a greater proportion of women than men study English, modern languages and social studies (Equal Opportunities Commission, 1998b). Rolfe (1999) highlights a key consequence of such choices: differences in pay. Whilst an apprentice in information technology may command £140 per week, and an engineering apprentice £115, a trainee hairdresser might receive as little as £62 per week. On average, women working full time earn only 80 per cent of the average hourly earnings of men who work full time, and only 72 per cent of their average weekly earnings (Equal Opportunities Commission, 1998a). The Equal Opportunities Commission attributes this 'pay gap', first, to the different occupations pursued by men and women and, second, to men's earnings being higher on average when men and women are in the same occupation (Equal Opportunities Commission, 1998a,b). Women are also more likely than men to be dependent on social security benefits. In May 1996 women comprised 54 per cent of the 5.5 million claimants on Income Support. Differential access to pensions extends the income gap into old age. In 1995 men aged 65–74 had an average income of £167 per week, women in the same age group averaged just £92 per week (Equal Opportunities Commission, 1998d). Children make a very real difference. While 94 per cent of men with children aged 4 or under are in work, only 54 per cent of women in the same circumstances are economically active (Equal Opportunities Commission, 1998c). Only recently have child care and other caring roles been recognised as unrewarded tasks, but the differences in income and opportunity have in no real way been redressed.

Ethnicity

The resources gap found between men and women is also to be found between white and black. British Labour Force Survey data show that average hourly earnings are higher for white men working full time than for men from ethnic minority groups. Pakistani and Bangladeshi men and women fare particularly badly in comparison with their respective counterparts in all other ethnic groups (Labour Force Survey 1994/5 quoted in Equal Opportunities Commission, 1998a). Beyond wealth, however, there are three further kinds of inequality which are pertinent here: institutional racism, access to employment, and access to appropriate goods and services.

One of the key concerns in recent times has been institutional racism, and though the phenomenon may be widespread, particular attention has fallen on the police force due to the Lawrence Inquiry. Briefly, in 1993 Stephen Lawrence was stabbed to death in Eltham in London. In July, 1997, the Home Secretary (Jack Straw) set up a public inquiry headed by Sir William Macpherson. One of the key findings of the enquiry was that the police investigation had been hampered by institutional racism. The Stephen Lawrence report

(Home Office, 1999: ch. 6, para. 34) defined institutional racism as:

> the collective failure of an organisation to provide an appropriate and pro-
> fessional service to people because of their colour, culture, or ethnic origin.
> It can be seen or detected in processes, attitudes and behaviour which
> amount to discrimination through unwitting prejudice, ignorance, thought-
> lessness and racist stereotyping which disadvantage minority ethnic
> people.

Where structural discrimination exists, certain groups are disadvantaged within the organisation concerned. Drawing on the example
of the National Health Service, many pieces of research have illumi-
nated discrimination in several aspects. So, for example, Abbasi
(1998) summarised a wide variety of evidence which revealed that
medical school selection was discriminatory. More specifically,
Esmail *et al.* (1995) examined rates of acceptance into medical
school and discovered that whilst there was little difference in rates
of acceptance between white and black applicants with excellent 'A'
level results, white students with lower 'A' level scores seemed to
have a greater chance of being admitted than applicants from ethnic
minority communities with similarly lower scores. In other research,
Esmail and Everington (1997, 1993) revealed discrimination against
Asian doctors applying for employment, and Esmail *et al.* (1998)
have discovered systematic racial discrimination in the allocation of
distinction awards to doctors. From these findings *inter alia*, Esmail
(1997: 618) concludes that the NHS is subject to institutional racism,
and that action is needed to secure the basics of good practice in
equal opportunities in order to 'challenge the system using the established legislative framework ... more openness and transparency are
essential'.

Apart from access to work, what of access to appropriate welfare
services? Do these take account of cultural diversity in their clients?
There are examples of policy and practice in both health and social
services which point to insensitivity to the needs of members of ethnic minorities in matters of food preparation, diet, rules regarding religious observance and the separation of the sexes (Gazdar, 1997;
Blakemore and Boneham, 1994; Pearson, 1986). For example, Ahmad
(1992, quoted in Drake, 1999) cites two cases. In one, a girl was made
to wear a nightdress throughout the day because her respite carers did
not know how to put on her 'ethnic clothing'. In the second, a black
elderly man in a residential home was labelled 'violent' by the staff

for refusing to eat bacon and throwing his plate from the table: his religion forbade the consumption of pork.

Age

There is evidence of discrimination in access to income and services according to age. With regard to income, many Western states have artificial cut-off points, nominated ages on reaching which workers must then retire. For many in Britain, at 65 a trap shuts. In certain occupations (especially low-paid jobs) retirement is compulsory, but it is also in the low-pay sector that private pensions are few and far between. Those who attracted low pay during their working lives are likely to receive state pension incomes far below the wages they commanded whilst at work. As a result, state pension policies leave many elderly people in vulnerable circumstances (Drake, 1998). Walker (1982a) has shown that poverty in old age is particularly related to class. Walker (1986, 1980) estimates that about two-thirds of Britain's 6 million pensioners live in, or on the margins of, poverty. Far from providing enough money for a comfortable old age, the basic state pension is so low that a considerable number of elderly people qualify for additional monies from those parts of the social security system (Income Support) normally reserved for the poorest members of society.

Beyond income, there is other evidence that older people may have poorer access to some other kinds of services, including the National Health Service (Age Concern, 1999a). A major survey for Age Concern conducted by Gallup found that one in twenty people over 65 had been refused treatment, and one in ten believed they had received different treatment since reaching their fiftieth birthday. Amongst many other kinds of example, Age Concern (1999b) reported instances of older people whose condition deteriorated so much while waiting for hip replacement operations that they became unfit for surgery.

A society may recognise that discrimination against older people occurs, and that it is primarily a consequence of priorities that favour younger, economically active people. Such a state may choose to ignore the inequity, and continue to sustain that position. Alternatively, it might seek to produce policies designed to overcome both discrimination and poverty, first, by helping low-paid workers to increase their pension provision and making retirement age a more

movable feast, and, second, by preventing age from being a criterion
in the allocation of resources by service providers.

Disability

Overall, disabled people represent about 14 per cent of the total population. In 1986 there were about 6.2 million adult disabled people in
Britain, 3.65 million men and 2.55 million women, and there were
some 360,000 disabled children. By extrapolation, George (1996)
suggests that today the figure for the total number of disabled adults
may have reached 6.6 millions. In the UK, very many disabled people
are (more or less permanently) absent from the world of work, few are
employees, even fewer are owners of businesses (Barnes, 1991). Only
about one-third of the disabled men, and even fewer, just 29 per cent
of disabled women have jobs (Martin *et al.*, 1989). We may compare
these levels to the equivalent measures for the employment of non-
disabled adults. In 1996 about 77 per cent of non-disabled people had
work, as against 32 per cent of disabled people (Sly, 1996). The figures have remained fairly constant over the 1990s (see for example,
Lonsdale, 1990). There is substantial evidence, then, that both the
level and the duration of unemployment amongst disabled people
have been consistently higher than those experienced by non-disabled
people (Hyde, 1996; Glendinning, 1991; Clark and Hirst, 1989; Hirst,
1987; Lonsdale, 1986; Townsend, 1979). Moreover, Barnes's (1991)
evidence suggests that even those who do have employment are less
likely than their non-disabled counterparts to occupy well-rewarded
posts. The average weekly wage of disabled male workers represents
only 81 per cent of the average enjoyed by non-disabled males
(Hansard, 6th June, 1989, col. 69) and Berthoud *et al.* (1993) highlight a direct connection between the severity of impairment and the
level of unemployment. More recent data from Blackaby *et al.* (1998)
explain that the great majority of disabled people earn less than their
non-disabled counterparts primarily because they occupy jobs
demanding fewer skills and qualifications, and confirm Barnes's contention that they have less access to the more professional and well-
paid posts. Indeed, disabled people tend to earn less than non-disabled
people even when they are doing similar (or even identical) jobs
(Martin and White, 1988). Generally, however, as shown in Table 6.1,
the work undertaken by disabled people tends to be less skilled than
that of their non-disabled counterparts, leading to the suggestion that,

Table 6.1 People in employment by social class (based on occupation) and whether disabled, 1996, Great Britain

Socio-economic group	Disabled (%)	Non-disabled (%)
Professional	4	6
Intermediate	26	31
Skilled (non-manual)	20	23
Skilled (manual)	23	20
Partly-skilled	20	15
Unskilled	7	5

Source: *Labour Market Trends*, September 1998, p. 422, table 8: People in employment by social class (based on occupation) and whether disabled. Data drawn from the 'Labour Force Survey', Office for National Statistics. © Crown Copyright, 1998

even when they have work, many disabled people are 'underemployed' (RADAR, 1993; Walker, 1982b).

The several examples I have just reviewed indicate that certain groups in society fare less well than others in commanding opportunities and resources. It is hardly credible to suppose that in their tens and hundreds of thousands, women, members of ethnic minority communities, elderly and disabled people have chosen voluntarily and spontaneously to subordinate themselves and their interests to allow other groups of citizens (predominantly white males) to stand pre-eminent in society's most powerful and influential positions. Is it not far more likely that their absence from such positions is caused by social structures rather than by individual volition?

Writers such as Kandola *et al.* (1995) and Behrens and Auluck (1993) suggest that a key step, and much more fruitful approach, would be to recognise that a diverse society, and, in particular, a diverse workforce, demands policies which value that diversity and so encourage equal opportunities and anti-discriminatory practice.

Potential policy responses to diversity

I have said that a government may respond to an increasingly diverse society in a number of ways. First, it may try to ignore differences altogether and seek to impose on all, irrespective of their cultural, ethnic or personal conditions, acceptance of prevailing values and norms.

It is possible that these values and norms may have been drawn from, and receive the support of, a very large section of the population. But equally, they may emerge from, and serve the interests of, a quite small but very powerful clique that controls the conduits of government.

Another possibility (the first was to try to impose uniformity irrespective of differences) is that the state may attempt to bring about change by reconfiguring the social and political environment. The purpose here would be to accommodate a variety of values and norms, including those of less powerful sub-groups in the population. Environmental change may be *universal* and radical, exchanging one set of values for another, or *piecemeal*, responding to specific matters in limited areas of policy and in closely targeted or defined ways. Finally, a government and various sub-groups may compromise so that all parties undertake change. Within an agreed measure of devolution a state may release some aspects of social and political control, but sub-groups may also give up certain desiderata and instead acquiesce in some measure to prevailing values and rules. The choice of strategy and the extent of change could, of course, have profound impacts on citizens' lives. Let us examine in more detail each of the options I have just outlined.

The imposition of uniformity

Recalling Lukes's (1974) account of the exercise of power, a governing group may be sufficiently powerful to bring its own values to universal acceptance, thereby subjugating other groups' values and interests. Colonisation, at least in the physical sense of the word, is an instrument identified more with the nineteenth century than with the twentieth. It is doubtful whether modern democratic states would choose outright tyranny as a way of reconciling competing social values in the future. It may be, however, that the empire-building of Victorian times has been replaced by a cultural imperialism of a different kind, in which the 'weapons' are tourism, global industries and worldwide communication systems such as the internet. And it may be that as the world gets smaller the threat to totalitarian values within certain states increases (see for example Giddens, 1999).

The acceptance and valuing of diversity

Apart from a tyrannical response, I outlined two other potential strategies with regard to diversity. First, a government may adopt principles which accommodate widely divergent values in the population. The benefit of this approach lies in the ability to develop very detailed policies producing different impacts for different groups. On the other hand, governments may embrace principles which restrict the scope of policy to a central core acceptable to all the diverse constituents of society, and then devolve powers and produce differential responses where there are areas of contention. In this way, none would suffer adverse impacts as a result of policy implementation. In either of these techniques ('divergence' or 'core and cluster' policy-making), there are difficulties to be overcome. For example, although the former, much more detailed approach might respond more sensitively to the values and norms of each separate sub-group, differential treatment may itself be discriminatory and give rise to charges of unfairness. We may also ponder just how much fragmentation is possible before a state may find it difficult to survive at all as a unitary entity. There are limits to federal or devolved approaches to policy-making. In the latter (core and cluster) approach, values may differ so greatly between sub-groups that they occupy little common ground, leading, as a result, to vitiated and ineffective policies. How, then, may governments meet the challenge of legislating for continuously changing societies of diverse populations?

A mixed response to diversity

One possible answer is a balance in approaches to diversity. As I suggested earlier in the book, minorities may need to recognise that within any democracy a government has a mandate given by a majority of those who voted. This does not mean, however, that a government is empowered to ride roughshod over the rights of minorities, but it does suggest that acceptance of core prevailing values may be necessary for a society to remain whole. The amount of diversity, therefore, will have implications for the viability of a society. When differences between groups in a population become too large, states may shatter into smaller and dissimilar territorial, ethnic and cultural administrations. To avoid such a dramatic outcome, some states have adopted devolved or federal patterns of government. For some, negotiation of change has resulted in large societal shifts. For others, the location of change has been within minority groups themselves. The key determinant will be the relative power and influence of the state vis-à-vis its various parts. Power imbalance (whether in one direction or the other) will tend to make the weaker entity the focus of most of the change for most of the time. Only where there is a balance of power may we expect to see similar amounts of compromise on both sides. The process of accommodating diversity is made the more difficult by pressures external to the entire process. For example, nation states are themselves sub-groups of a global society. Of the 100 most powerful economic entities, only 49 are nation states, the remaining 51 are international companies (World Bank, 2000; Fortune, 2000). Equally, minority groups may have allegiances to global religions or to ethnic groupings living in territories distant from the society in question. Clearly, then, responding to diversity and difference is not merely a matter of academic interest. In seeking to bring about real changes, the New Labour government has applied some of these ideas to policy formulation in the contemporary British context. It is to the application of ideas of diversity and difference that I now turn.

Policy as an instrument of change

Social policies may guide (or resist) changes in response to increasing cultural and social plurality within a population. Where policy principles acknowledge difference, but maintain values which serve the interests of one particular social group over others, this is likely to constrain diversity and retard change. However, where policy principles recognise difference and allow for the development of *fair* kinds of inequalities, then such policies will permit plurality and choice, and will promote diversity.

I have argued that the identification of policies and practices which promote diversity have been central to the writing of authors such as Kandola *et al.* (1995), Kandola (1993), Parekh (1992), and Kandola and Fullerton (1984). All of these authors stress that policies must recognise and respond appropriately to differences between people arising from their gender, ethnicity, age and physiology. They also recognise that different policy responses are likely to lead to different kinds of services. However, the key point is that factors such as gender, ethnicity, age and disability should not lead to policies and practices that differ in the quality or level of response accorded to individuals. In other words, the interplay of any differences should allow for the development of diverse (as opposed to uniform) policy responses, but, at the same time, such differences must not promote unfair inequalities (and therefore injustices) in the treatment of (some) citizens as a direct consequence of such policies.

To return to an earlier example, recognising that the mobility of some people (wheelchair users) depends on wheels rather than feet, equality of opportunity is maintained by policies which produce vehicles configured to carry wheelchair users as well as passengers whose mobility is, so to speak, 'foot-based'. Notwithstanding the implementation of the Disability Discrimination Act (1995), the great majority of public transport in Britain fails to serve disabled people. This failure demonstrates the further point that social policies are formulated by, and thus accord with, the interests of those in power, and disabled people in Britain have, up to now, found political participation and influence particularly difficult to achieve (Drake, 1999; Fry, 1987).

There is a broader point to be made here. If a governing group prefers a particular skin colour, or is weighted towards a particular gender, or has specific religious or secular beliefs, or supports particular family-based rituals and structures, then it is possible – more than this, it is exceedingly likely – that the social policies it creates will favour these predispositions and interests. At worst, such a government may be wholly intolerant of difference, may, for example, encourage racism, stimulate homophobic attitudes, propagate gender stereotyping or produce an economic and social underclass. Policies which reflect and support the social, economic and political characteristics of one group at the expense of others are discriminatory. They produce unfair inequalities and, in so doing, are (in Rawls's sense) unjust. Such policies arise, at least in part, because a group privileged by them wishes to maintain its advantages. It thus seeks to ensure that the policy montage continues to be sympathetic to its own interests. The onus will be on policies which maintain the status quo and resist change, or which go further by enhancing even more the dominant group's own privileges. How could such circumstances as these be overcome?

If certain policy principles lead to perceived injustices, it is these injustices that have been at the root of pressure for change. Where a state has failed to respond to calls for change, such pressures have frequently built up, eventually to explode in civil commotion and violence (Vogler, 1991; Gifford, 1986; Harris *et al.*, 1983). But at a less dramatic level, methods of change have imbued the policies and practices of many kinds of social organisations. In recent years social institutions have devoted much attention to the *management* of change through connecting two approaches: equality of opportunity and 'managing diversity'. The aim has been to remove injustices by basing policy and practice decisions on intrinsic criteria instead of extrinsic factors. As authors such as Kandola *et al.* (1995), Kandola (1993), Parekh (1992), and Kandola and Fullerton (1984) all point out, there are benefits not only for individuals, but also for governments and companies in such an approach. For example, in the world of work it is not merely fairer, it is more *efficient* to employ someone for their capacity to do the job than for, let us say, their skin colour. In a multicultural society, the company with a diverse workforce is more likely to be successful than one restricted to a particular ethnic group. Policies which respect and accommodate a diverse society will tend to be inclusive, they will encourage participation in government and social administration. They will foster permissive instead of restrictive regimes and allow for innovation and expression. Policy principles based on diversity will optimise liberty for all groups and use education to equip people for citizenship. Here, the open society is preferable to the closed mind.

Conclusion

In this chapter I have been concerned with the effects of a changing world on social policy, and, in its turn, of social policy in a changing world. I have argued that societies may either constrain diversity by reinforcing the values and privileges of existing dominant groups, or may enhance diversity by encouraging equality of opportunity and pluralism. In particular, the kinds of policy that governments put in place will have a direct effect upon the quality of citizenship that a population can enjoy. It is, therefore, to the concept of citizenship that I now turn.

7

Citizenship

In the book so far there has been a leitmotif, a sub-theme, which has run through the analysis without being overtly recognised. This theme is the constitution of citizenship. Citizenship mediates interactions between individuals and the state. Our understanding of the concept is important in shaping the contours of government and law, for the creation of social policies, and for the impacts of policy on individuals. Writers such as Phillips (1991), Young (1990) and Lister (1997) argue that universal citizenship can only be achieved where all members of a society participate equally in coming to a working definition that specifies boundaries, privileges and duties. In the first half of the chapter, therefore, I elaborate four prerequisites for citizenship: membership; participation; entitlements, and obligations. In the second half, I assess the reciprocal influence of citizenship over the formulation of social policy and, in turn, the influence of social policy on the quality of citizenship.

Though many have made the attempt, the concept of 'citizenship' has proved difficult to pin down (Kymlicka and Norman, 2000; Lehning and Weale, 1997; Oommen, 1997; Demaine and Entwistle, 1996; Einhorn *et al.,* 1996; Pixley, 1993; Bock and James, 1992; Roche, 1992; Mead, 1986; Marshall, 1950). Indeed, the degree of variation in meaning has left Gunsteren (1998: 11) rather doubtful about the possibility of providing any useful definition at all:

> Citizenship is not an eternal essence but a cultural artifact. It is what people make of it. Like language, it depends on, and changes with, usage. Changes in political regimes and agendas usually entail changes in the uses and meanings of citizenship.

Gunsteren concludes that the nearest one can get to the act of definition is to marshal historical uses of the term in order to map out

119

a 'field of meanings'. While accepting that the term exhibits all the mutability that Gunsteren propounds, it is still possible to take a less pessimistic view. What is clear about the various attempts to define citizenship is that all are agreed that the word is intended to express a relationship between individuals and governance (Kymlicka and Norman, 2000; Marshall, 1992; Roche, 1992). Furthermore, our understanding of 'citizenship' in any particular context depends on the elucidation of four key aspects of that relationship: membership; participation; entitlements, and obligations.

Defining citizenship

Membership

For a person to be a citizen, he or she must be a 'member' of a particular state (Turner, 1993). Membership is usually betokened by certain kinds of relationship in which individuals and states each acknowledge the other (for example, through the payment of taxes or the protection of the law). Turner (1993: 2, 3) therefore defines membership as a set of practices – juridical, political, economic and cultural – which define a person as a competent member of society. Citizenship is 'essentially about the nature of social membership within modern political collectivities'. Mendus (1989) stresses the need not only for the actuality of membership but also for the perception of membership: people need to feel that they belong.

Participation

Mere belonging, however, does not, of itself, confer citizenship. Membership is a reciprocal status. A person will not only be subject to the laws and customs of a state, but may also, as Aristotle tells us in the *Politics*, take some part in the administration of justice and may be appointed to office, or participate in the election of others. For Voet (1998: 137), participation in the running of government is the key aspect of citizenship. She argues that:

> A full citizen in its most complete sense is someone who participates in legislation or decision-making in public affairs. It concerns participation through which one reflects upon the desirable new character of society

and through which one rejuvenates society by cooperating with other people. It is participation whereby one discusses common affairs with others, reflects upon the common good, learns to bear responsibility, to judge and to decide.

Where a person lacks citizenship, this may come about through encountering barriers to participation. Constraints may be found either in prevailing social norms, values and attitudes or in more tangible, physical or environmental conditions. Equally, the adopted definition of citizenship may itself prevent equality of treatment, membership and participation for some individuals.

For example, Phillips (1991) and Young (1990) insist that citizenship has to take account of biological differences between men and women instead of treating both sexes under the generic label 'human'. In their submission, the term 'human' often masks an actuality that operates in favour of maleness. Lister (1997: 195) takes the argument further in asking whether 'the concept of citizenship, born within the context of a masculine society can be "woman friendly"?'. She argues that it cannot, and that what is needed is a feminist reconstruction of citizenship. To include women it is, Lister argues, necessary to expose the current 'false universalism' of the concept and build a new principle which includes a gender analysis of difference so as to create a 'differentiated universalism'. Lister seeks a pluralistic concept so that 'a woman-friendly citizenship is thus rooted in difference' (p. 198). Such a concept requires far greater fluidity between what until now has been the male, public, independent sphere and the female, domestic and dependent sphere. Lister contends that the difficulty in bringing about change is that the institutions which hold the greatest influence in defining citizenship are still dominated by men. Citizenship, then, must be concerned with the inclusion of individuals in a society so that together they may agree its structures, institutions, mores and norms. The outcome desired of such a process is the accommodation of plurality and difference.

If the prevailing definition of citizenship may exclude some, it is equally true that other, marginalised groups may find it hard to get their own values and beliefs accepted and they may consequently face stigmatisation (Lukes, 1974; Goffman, 1964). Other barriers to citizenship may arise from linguistic and semantic exclusion. Some groups, for example medicine and the law, have their own special languages explicitly designed to exclude others (Cohen, 1985). Words may be 'hijacked' and redefined in accord with prevailing philosophies, so that the meaning of participation itself can be diluted to the level of mere tokenism (Arnstein, 1969). Physical structures can also become barriers to citizenship. The built environment remains problematic for people who are deaf, blind or use wheelchairs (Drake, 1999; Imrie, 1996; Imrie and Wells, 1993; Swain *et al.,* 1993). Social structures, procedures and operations may constitute barriers, as may the distribution of resources. Some commentators (Dean and Taylor Gooby, 1992; Andrews and Jacobs, 1990) argue that poverty (and the stigma it may attract) can serve to undermine citizenship: 'To be poor is to endure conditional citizenship' (Golding in Lister, 1990: vii).

To give an example of how citizenship for some may be hindered by our conceptualisation of differences between individuals, the contemporary ethos of social welfare is based predominantly on a 'personal tragedy' or medical model of disability (Drake, 1999; Barnes *et al.,* 1999; Priestley, 1999; Oliver, 1990; Abberley, 1987). It is assumed that disabled people require special and separate services to compensate them for what are seen as individual deficits and incapacities. Compensatory activities are described as 'care', and interventions ('therapy') are aimed at changing the physiology or cognition of an individual rather than the physical and social environment (Priestley, 1999; Symonds and Kelly, 1998; Drake, 1996a; Oliver, 1990). Such a model militates against the formulation of policies and practices informed by an alternative account of disability known as the 'social model' (Drake, 1999; Barnes *et al.,* 1999; Oliver, 1990; Abberley, 1987). The social model sees disability as a consequence of society failing, through both its construction and operation, to serve all its citizens. People are rendered 'disabled' because the contours of society are shaped to accommodate persons of the prevailing physiological and cognitive design ('the able-bodied') rather than a range of others. Were the social model of disability to be fully accepted and incorporated in policy-making, it would require a wholesale reorientation of the work of statutory and voluntary welfare agencies away from the notion of the 'disabled individual', and towards the idea of a 'disabling society' (Barnes *et al.,* 1999; Oliver, 1996; Swain *et al.,* 1993). The overriding goal would be the achievement of legislative, institutional and social change in order to render all aspects of community life accessible to all citizens, including disabled citizens (Drake, 1999; Oliver and Barnes, 1998; Campbell and Oliver, 1996; Barnes, 1991). In the circumstances I have just described, it is only changes in environmental structures and the parameters of society that would allow marginalised groups access to the rights and privileges enjoyed by other individuals in their experience of citizenship. But more than this, the necessary social and environmental changes would also redefine citizenship itself. Exclusion, on the other hand, may render marginalised groups rebellious, quiescent or apathetic (Gaventa, 1980; Crenson, 1971).

Bradshaw and Holmes (1989) have documented the apathy that prevailed amongst poor families in Tyne and Wear in the face of unremitting exclusion from work and other key functions of society. Crenson (1971), Lukes (1974) and Gaventa (1980) have recognised the potency of such quiescence: a product, they argue, of sustained and unremitting powerlessness. Indeed, quiescence can become so strong that people may even come to maintain their own powerlessness and so oppress themselves (Gaventa, 1980; Freire, 1972; Gramsci, 1971). Alienation, apathy and quiescence thus constitute important symptoms in the detection of social exclusion and the absence of citizenship.

In my own study (Drake, 1996a, 1996b, 1994), several disabled people were unfamiliar with the notion of participation, and many of those that were remained apathetic towards it. For some, however, the recognition that they occupied a position of sustained powerlessness was leading them to reject not only the traditional welfare state, but also the whole notion of disability and its bedfellow 'charity'. In particular they chose not to struggle for power within existing voluntary groups, deeming them largely irrelevant to their requirements. Instead, many users were joining agencies *of* rather than *for* disabled people and saw the battle for citizenship as a political, rather than personal, struggle (Campbell and Oliver, 1996; Drake, 1992; Pagel, 1988; Barton, 1986).

In sum, then, two key determinants of the quality of citizenship are membership of, and participation in, society. Where these are absent, there is a danger of exclusion and disaffection resulting in either rebellion or acquiescence. I return to the matter of exclusion from citizenship later in the chapter in discussing the impacts of social policy.

Entitlements

Membership and participation are *necessary* elements of citizenship, but they are not *sufficient* ones. Many writers have contended that there is more to being a citizen than simply being one of a group and being able to take a full part in the shaping and development of a society (Kymlicka and Norman, 2000; Lehning and Weale, 1997; Oommen, 1997; Demaine and Entwistle, 1996; Einhorn *et al.,* 1996; Pixley, 1993; Bock and James, 1992; Roche, 1992; Mead, 1986; Marshall, 1950). Beyond this foundation, scholars have proposed that membership confers certain entitlements and exacts certain duties. Some authors have tended to explore the question of rights and entitlements (Tawney, 1964; Marshall, 1950), while others have given more attention to clarifying duties and obligations (Mead, 1986; Tebbit, 1986). By and large, it has been the concern of those primarily on the left of the political spectrum to emphasise the rights and entitlements of citizenship. This approach is perhaps most famously represented by authors such as Tawney (1964) and Marshall (1992). In Marshall's *Citizenship and Social Class*, originally written in 1950, the fulfilment of citizenship depended on a person's access to civil, political and social rights. By *civil rights* Marshall was referring to 'rights necessary for individual freedom' and which might therefore cover such things as freedom of speech, thought and faith, including access to information, and the right to freedom of association and organisation. This area of rights would also include equality before the law and (p. 8) 'the right to own property and conclude valid contracts'.

Earlier in the chapter I discussed participation as a key requirement, and Marshall used the term *political rights* to denote that aspect of citizenship. These rights included the right to participate in the exercise of political power as a member of a governing body or as an elector and, therefore, the right to vote and seek political office in free elections. Finally, Marshall elaborated a third class of rights, *social rights.* Here he included (p. 8):

> the right to a modicum of economic welfare and security [and] the right to share to the full in the social heritage and to live the life of a civilised being according to the standards prevailing in the society.

Turner (1993: 7) has supplemented Marshall's initial three classes of rights with three more, all of which accentuate the 'social rights' element of Marshall's analysis. Turner postulates *welfare rights* which go beyond Marshall's notion of a modicum of economic welfare and security. For Turner, welfare rights 'involve some principle of redistribution' and they therefore have the capacity to promote an 'egalitarian transformation of social hierarchies'. What Turner is saying is that entitlements may go beyond the idea of rights within a *given* sociopolitical structure to include *changes to that structure itself.*

Second, Marshall is criticised for a failure to deal with *economic rights*. Turner points in particular to the power that accrues to workers where they enjoy the right of controlling the enterprises in which they are employed. Finally, drawing on Parsons's (1971, 1966) idea of cultural citizenship, Turner (1993: 7) proposes the notion of *educational rights* which he contends are necessary in order that people may 'participate in the complex culture of a particular society'.

In similar vein, Hindess (1993: 25) has stressed the acute importance of social rights as critical elements of citizenship, arguing that without them 'the formal equality of civil and political rights will be somewhat restricted'. For Hindess, civil and political rights can only have meaning and significance where a citizen can command sufficient resources (mental as well as material) to exercise those rights. Esping-Anderson (1990: 21) makes a similar point, expressed in the context of economics. For him, the 'outstanding criterion of social rights must be the degree to which they permit people to make their living standards independent of pure market forces'.

This view is supported by many other writers, such as Twine (1994), who argues that social rights protect people from the vagaries of the labour market. Both Gould (1988) and Twine (1994: 105) assert that citizens are entitled to 'social resources' such as health and education 'not only for economic efficiency but also to participate effectively in furthering their own and other people's civil and political rights, to further their life projects'. Finally, Roche (1992) argues that the nature of social rights is changing in response to political restructuring and the attenuation of the nation state through both global and internal forces. For Roche, social rights must extend beyond welfare and the workplace to respond to the potential ecological dangers of new technology and the rights of future generations in sharing and managing the finite resources of the earth.

Assertions of social rights do not, of course, go uncontested. As Roche (1992) points out, some strands of neo-conservatism deny the existence of social rights entirely, whilst New Right variants emphasise duties over rights and seek to reduce state involvement in welfare. Similarly, Saunders (1993) has argued that the fulfilment of 'social rights' through state provision is both inefficient and dependency creating. He argues that two-thirds of the British population is now in a position to exercise choice in purchasing from the private sector what were previously public services such as pensions and schooling. For the residuum, Saunders (1993: 68) contends that

> vouchers or cash transfers are inherently superior to state provision in
> kind ... as a means for enabling effective consumer choice and accountability.

Saunders is not, therefore, against the notion that citizens have a
right to education and health per se, but he is against the idea of state
monopoly in the supply of these things. Moreover, he is happy to
accept as legitimate an unequal distribution of such resources on the
basis that patterns of distribution that result from a free market can
be thought of as being neither moral nor immoral: free markets are
amoral. Saunders does not, however, deal with Winkler's (1987) criticism that whilst consumers may choose between different 'brands'
they do not get a seat on the board and decide what is to be put on
the shelves. For her, citizenship is a matter of control rather than
choice. Further, Saunders accepts that the encouragement of individ-
ualistic ambition that lies at the heart of a competitive free market
can have a corrosive effect on moral society by diminishing a citizen's sense of social obligation. However, he contends that states
cannot impose moral behaviour either, rather, morality is, he concludes, grounded in voluntarism.

Clearly, then, questions of entitlement and rights are as controversial as questions of justice. For Saunders, citizenship is primarily
about the protection of individuals' autonomy. Before leaving the
question of entitlements and moving on to discuss the notion of
obligations to the state, it is fair to make the point that many on the
moderate right wing of politics would accept as part and parcel of
citizenship many of the social and political rights we have just discussed. At the same time it can be said of radical authors that,
notwithstanding their conviction that rights are fundamental to citizenship, very few would deny that citizens also owe responsibilities
to the state. At the extremes, however, we may see that despots and
tyrants of both left and right have historically empathised much more
with the duties of citizenship than the rights bestowed by it (if they
have given any thought to the concept at all).

Obligations

To be a citizen is to owe certain duties or obligations to the state. Of
course, these vary from country to country and may change over
time. In contemporary Britain (unless allowed exemption, for example by dint of one's age) such obligations may typically include the

payment of taxes, the undertaking of jury service, or (in times of war) service in the armed forces (Dunn, 1980; Walzer, 1970).

So, just as authors on the left of the political spectrum may stress the rights and entitlements of citizenship, those on the right, such as Mead (1986) and Tebbit (1986) tend to emphasise a variety of duties and obligations to the state. Most recently this idea has been encapsulated in the term 'active citizen' (Major, 1999, 1997). Andrews (1991: 12) reminds us that though the modern notion of 'active citizenship' was developed by (*inter alia*) Douglas Hurd and John Major, it echoed a tradition rooted in Victorian values 'in which the virtues of self-help were combined with moral obligation to help worthy causes'. The active citizen was someone who did his or her duty by, for example, joining the local neighbourhood watch scheme, giving blood, or working as a volunteer for charity (Major, 1999, 1997). Though the service of others is the tangible outward sign of active citizenship, the key duty identified by Conservative thinkers and politicians is the upkeep of oneself and one's family in order to avoid becoming a burden on the state (Thatcher, 1993; Walters, 1986). A further strand of Major's thinking on citizenship concerned the relationship between public services and individuals. In his view the service provider had dominated that relationship and his aim was to tilt the balance towards the consumer by forcing the public sector to enumerate the rights of its users and to publish standards of performance against which services could be measured (Prior *et al.*, 1995). However, some earlier, more general criticisms of the privatising of public services is pertinent in evaluating Major's notion of citizenship. Winkler (1987), questioned both the degree of genuine participation involved and the rights actually conferred, whilst Taylor (1992) argued that the introduction of Charters could amount to a method through which any evaluative focus could be switched towards the local running of public services and away from central government, thus deflecting closer scrutiny of policy aims and intentions.

According to an observer's political values, then, citizenship may be defined primarily in terms of the rights commanded by individuals, or by the obligations owed by them, but most modern analyses of citizenship recognise the concept as fundamentally reciprocal (Prior *et al.*, 1995). The term describes a mutual relationship: citizens have *both* rights *and* obligations. A person's citizenship is damaged if rights are denied, but also if obligations go unfulfilled. In this vein, Scruton (1982) defines a citizen as being one who owes allegiance to, and receives protection from, a state. As Barry (in Plant, 1990: 49) has suggested:

> Citizenship requires that individuals be active and informed members of the community, capable of taking on its burdens as well as enjoying its benefits.

Citizenship and social policy

I have said that we may understand citizenship as having four constituent parts, all of which must be present in some degree for a person to be a citizen. These were: membership of a society, participation in its governance, entitlement to the rights it confers and readiness to fulfil the obligations it exacts. If any one of these four elements is entirely absent, it becomes difficult, perhaps impossible, to conceive of a person as a citizen. Without rights a person is as a slave or a prisoner. In failing to fulfil his or her obligations, a person becomes a pariah. On being refused membership, a person is an exile or an alien. Without participation in government, a person is disenfranchised and rendered powerless.

These elements are not 'all or nothing' phenomena. They can be matters of degree. To be exiled from society need not be a dramatic event, in the way that unpopular Athenians were ostracised from their beloved *polis*. In modern Britain, for example, disabled people are excluded by ill-designed offices, shops, buses and trains that prevent them in large numbers from participating in work or in society at large. They are exiled from certain leisure facilities by both prejudice and inaccessibility (Drake, 1999; Oliver and Barnes, 1998; Swain *et al.*, 1993; Barnes, 1991).

Marshall argues that one function of the welfare state is to limit the negative impacts of class differences on individual life chances, thereby enhancing an individual's commitment to society (Novak, 1988; Marshall, 1950). However, where inequalities become extreme, and the lack of equal opportunities is most severe, there may emerge groups of people who feel that their rights are being denied them and that, as a consequence, they owe no duties to (and may reject) the society and state from which they feel estranged (Mann, 1994; Brown, 1990; Gaventa, 1980; Cloward and Ohlin, 1960; Cohen, 1955). Of course, any evaluation of the accuracy of such claims is difficult. In a state which imprisoned people without trial, which used torture as an instrument of government, or which assassinated thinkers, writers and political dissidents, there would be a very stark sense indeed of the denial of rights and thus the negation of citizenship. But how ought we to regard, for example, an administrative change in the provision of a social security benefit or a reduction in the period for which it is paid? What of such intangibles as information withheld so that we do not hear about things with which, if we did know about them, we might certainly disagree? For example, is citizenship harmed by the 'non-intentional misleading of Parliament' by Ministers (Scott, 1996)? The cardinal point is this: through their aims, implementation or outcomes, social policies may enhance citizenship or retard it. They do so because social policies exert a very direct influence over the four key aspects we have just considered: the quality of social membership; opportunities to participate; access to entitlements, and the imposition of obligations.

Policy and law: impacts on membership, participation, entitlements and obligations

A government's policies, and the laws subsequently enacted, may confer or deny membership of a society. For example, a country's immigration laws may actively welcome people from other lands to settle as full citizens within its borders or may seek to exclude them (Dummett and Nicol, 1990; Grant and Martin, 1982). During the 1950s and 1960s Britain's industries were working at full capacity and more labour was needed than could be provided from the domestic population (Peach *et al.*, 1988). As a result, immigration was encouraged. Inflows from the West Indies peaked in the early 1960s and from the Indian sub-continent in 1968 (Lowe, 1993). In a more recent example, however, the aim was to restrict immigration. The British Nationality (Hong Kong) Act, 1990, restricted to only 50,000 the number of persons (and their immediate families) to whom full British passports might be granted. This left some 2–3 million Hong Kong residents without the right of British citizenship when the colony reverted to Chinese rule in July 1997 (Higgins, 1996a, 1996b; Smithers, 1996; Young, 1995).

We may draw on another international example to show how a government can deny citizenship to people even in their own native land. During the 1960s, the apartheid regime in South Africa attempted to transform the country's political geography by removing millions of people from designated white areas to black townships and homelands (Smith, 1982; Lemon, 1976; Baldwin, 1975). First, access to welfare and political rights was made dependent on state-manipulated ethnic identities; then, in 1976 the Transkei homeland was given its 'independence', to be followed over the next four years by Bophuthatswana, Ciskei and Venda (*Encyclopaedia Britannica*, 1997). These moves were clearly aimed at excluding black and other non-white populations from citizenship of the Republic of South Africa.

In the South African example, policy was highly visible, dramatic and *intentional*. Consider, however, a more subtle example. What quality of membership can be enjoyed in societies where there are sizeable inequalities in wealth? Though the poorest may formally be called citizens, it is possible that, where the disparities grow sufficiently large, some groups experience a degree of deprivation so great that they come to be thought of as a class apart (Mann, 1994; Dean and Taylor Gooby, 1992), devoid of the power to contribute to the creation of social norms and structures. Even though a state may have no malign intentions, poverty can, at the extreme, retard membership, deter participation and thus undermine citizenship (Brown, 1990; Andrews and Jacobs, 1990).

Earlier in the chapter I suggested that exclusion from citizenship may result in some measure of either rebellion or quiescence amongst marginalised groups (Gaventa, 1980; Crenson, 1971; Gramsci, 1971). Moreover, policies may have a major impact on the quality of citizenship that such groups encounter. Legislation may either encourage participation in governance or actually prevent it. For example, under British law, as in many other countries, prisoners are not allowed to vote in local or general elections. There are, however, other, more subtle barriers to participation in government and public life more generally. Fry (1987) has detailed the difficulties faced by disabled people of access to polling booths in order to vote, and Barnes (1991) has exposed the severe under-representation of disabled people in politics at both local and national level, whilst Drake (1999) has detailed their absence from large parts of the civil service and other administrative professions. It follows that social policies may be designed to remove the barriers faced by excluded sections of the population, or may instead reinforce those obstacles, or even add more to them. In the example I have just given, laws could allow disabled people to vote by mail or by proxy and could direct that polling stations must be accessible (see Barnes, 1991: 209–14 for a cogent analysis of these issues).

Social policies are crucial as instruments for extending, limiting or withdrawing entitlements and obligations. The entitlements of a citizen might include, for example, receiving the protection of the state, either through diplomatic services abroad or from the forces of law and order at home. A citizen will have political and legal entitlements such as the right to vote or the right to a fair trial. There may be welfare entitlements through a system of social security benefits and pensions, and entitlements to other services such as education and health. In sum, then, social policies are important for their role in shaping the contours of a welfare state and in determining the purposes and extent of social insurance and allied services.

Policies and their related legislation also set out the duties and obligations of citizens in any particular society. British law covers such matters as jury service, liability to taxation, and service in the armed forces. Duties may be light and few or many and arduous. Obligations vary according to the circumstances in which citizens find themselves. So, for example, an elderly person may be excused call-up into the armed forces at time of war. There is, however, a contentious question about the reciprocity of entitlements and obligations. There is a continuing debate in both Britain and America concerning the notion of 'workfare'. At the heart of the debate stands the question as to whether – as an obligation of citizenship – social security claimants should be compelled to do work in the local community in return for their benefits (Walker, 1991; Digby, 1989). It is over issues like these that the constitution of citizenship is, perhaps, most fiercely debated.

Conclusions

Citizenship is one of the most important terms used to enunciate the relationship between individuals and the state. To be a citizen involves some recognition of membership, some sort of participation in the processes of government, the possession of certain rights and entitlements, and the obligation to perform certain duties. As Gunsteren warned us at the outset, there is no single conceptualisation of citizenship. In accordance with his or her particular values, an observer will nominate different qualities for, and different limits to, each of these four components. Some commentators will be concerned to specify many and various entitlements of citizenship which the state must acknowledge and protect. Other writers will seek to minimise the role of the state and instead emphasise the duties an individual must perform if he or she desires to be counted a 'citizen'. Some will want to define citizenship as a direct and intimate involvement in collective government, others will eulogise autonomy and choice in a market place free of government interference.

As we have seen, the particular stance which prevails at any specific time has consequences not only for the contours of citizenship in any particular society, but also for the profile of social policy in that society. The terms of membership and participation and the specification of entitlements and obligations will (potentially) have both positive and negative impacts on the lives of individuals. We have seen that the experience of citizenship may depend on matters so esoteric as where a person was born, the colour of his or her skin, his or her age, gender, religion, cognition or physiology. At the heart of the debate about citizenship stands the fundamental issue of the exercise of power. In the end, prevailing values determine which, if any, of an individual's characteristics will play a part in determining his or her access to (and experience of) citizenship. Though the constitutions of many democratic societies declare allegiance to the principle of equitable treatment, in reality individuals' experience of citizenship owes much to their personal circumstances, allegiances and backgrounds.

In the book so far, I have argued that the values and beliefs of those in government inform the principles from which social policies are derived. The precise contours of citizenship will be shaped by these policies, formed according to prevailing understandings of justice, and built on political values which may enhance or curtail individual liberties. Policies may encourage collective responses to social problems or promote individual self-reliance. They may defer to individual autonomy and leave well alone, or they may emphasise equality and redistribute wealth and opportunities. The outcomes of policy will depend on the principles held, the policies created, and the practices observed, and it is to the analysis of this process of policy realisation that I now turn.

8

Policy Analysis

The purpose of this chapter is to relate the theoretical ideas discussed earlier in the book to the analysis of social policy in the real world. There are three main sections. First, I review briefly some common and well-established approaches to social policy analysis. Second, I consider in more detail a number of essential analytical elements. Third, I use a specific example (a piece of housing legislation) to illustrate the application of these elements in the elucidation of policy.

Analysing social policies

Social policy research can take place at many levels. Some writers have emphasised the identification of principles and values, some the efficiency of implementation and practice, and others the outcomes and their consequences. Others still have sought to combine all of these ingredients in order to produce multifaceted analyses. So, for example, writers like Dye (1987) and Weiss (1972) are interested less in the initial selection of policy objectives than in the measurement of congruity between aims and outcomes. Dye (1987: 351) contends that policy research comprises the:

> objective, systematic, empirical examination of the effects [that] ongoing policies and public programmes have on their targets in terms of the goals they are meant to achieve.

Miller (1984) acknowledges the value of quantitative performance measurement yielded by 'scientific' techniques. However, his main concern is to develop a clear understanding of guiding principles. Miller's more judgemental stance accentuates the aims and impacts of policies and the values which underpin them. In sympathy with this approach, Guba and Lincoln (1987) have argued that it is appropriate for those on the receiving end of policy to participate fully in evaluative programmes.

Yet other writers (Parsons, 1995; Rist, 1995; Bobrow and Dryzek, 1987; Simon, 1969) seek to balance enquiry into policy implementation (efficiency) with an interrogation of policy objectives (aims). For example, Parsons (1995) identifies two distinct methods of review. First, he discusses policy analysis as a tool in the management of human resources (i.e. the elucidation of process). Second, he considers policy analysis as a rational project concerned with the appraisal of purposes. Like Miller, Parsons also distinguishes between the activities of *measurement* (determining success or failure in the achievement of intended and specified goals) and of *judgement* (assessing the desirability of the policy and its impacts). These various approaches need not, of course, be mutually exclusive. By bringing them together we may achieve a more comprehensive investigation of policy in its several parts: values and principles; purposes and implementation; practice and outcomes.

Analytical elements

Values and principles

The initial step in any analysis begins with values and principles. There are at least three pertinent questions here. First, what values and principles does a government use to guide the formulation of its policies? Second, what principles have been declared, or may be discerned by observation? Third, what is the scope of these principles, are they closely circumscribed within specific areas of action or do they enunciate more general objectives, above and beyond the substantive matters in hand? The first two questions are, perhaps, reasonably clear. The third may need further explanation. This final question is about the relationship between the general and the local or specific. Our aim is to know how far a policy has been formulated to pursue ambitions which lie outside an immediate area of interest – is there some grander political goal such as social justice or equality of opportunity – and how far its aims focus more tightly on a quite specific matter within some substantive area of concern (for example, a lifelong learning strategy). In reality, of course, it will almost always be true that both kinds of objective are involved. In the example I have just mooted, a government could work towards *both* equality of opportunity *and* a more skilled population, recognising education to be a major plank in the pursuit of equality of opportunity (Cosin *et al.*, 1989; Cole, 1989; Sanderson, 1987; Boudon, 1974; Silver, 1973). A government's overarching aims will depend to some extent on its perception of the values we discussed earlier in the book: justice; liberty; equality; rights, and duties. From any specific blend of these values there emerges a particular conceptualisation of citizenship.

At the most general level, policy purposes will be shaped by a government's concept of justice. Broadly, we may expect administrations which favour personal autonomy, independence and self-reliance to be sympathetic to Nozick's (1974) view of justice which has less to do with matters of equality or redistribution than with the fairness of transactions and interactions between people within a free market. On the other hand, parties subscribing to political doctrines which support mutual or collective governance may accord more closely with Rawls's (1972) concept of justice and its concern not only for fair contract and process, but also for the effects of outcomes. To discern a government's understanding of justice, there are tangible questions that we may ask of policy outcomes, for example:

- What inequalities, if any, arise ?
- Who benefits from these inequalities ?
- What privileges are afforded and to whom?
- Are the privileges attached to offices, or are they personally held?
- Who benefits from these privileges ?
- Who, if anyone, suffers as a result of the policy, and in what ways ?

Matters would be more complex under communitarian forms of governance because the realisation of justice would vary according to the specific areas of policy and specific levels of government we were investigating. The notion of justice may be different in each sphere of life (Walzer, 1983). It also follows that the concept of governance would, itself, be more variegated and multi-layered. Such a society might create several levels and forms of administration to reflect the plurality of groups within the population (Young, 1990).

Our analysis would also be concerned with liberty and equality. So, for example, we may expect to see the policies created by traditional right-wing parties emphasising individual autonomy and self-reliance, whereas policies promoted by parties on the traditional left might accentuate mutuality, equality and collectivity (Bulmer *et al.*, 1989). In more communitarian societies we may see a plurality of positions. Some aspects of policy could afford extensive individual liberty whereas others may entail closer patterns of equality.

Finally, our analysis of policy should consider the balance between entitlements and obligations. Some governments emphasise the duties of the citizen, others are sensitive to the question of rights. In our exploration of citizenship, we saw how many scholars view the relationship between the individual and the state as being a reciprocal one in which entitlements are counterbalanced by obligations (Jones, 1994; Twine, 1994). Policies, and the laws through which they are implemented, provide the specific contours of that relationship at any particular time. We may ask, therefore, whether a policy, or a change in policy, confers new or amended rights or imposes novel or modified obligations. We may also estimate the potential consequences, or assess the actual outcomes, of such changes.

In all but the most anarchic societies, rights and duties flow from policy implementation through the enactment of laws. These rights and obligations tell us something of the character of the state and define the quality of citizenship. Where individuals have excessive rights and few duties the state itself will be much weakened. Where the reverse is true and individuals have many duties but inadequate rights and protections, the state is likely to be oppressive or, at the extreme, autocratic and tyrannical.

For them to be realised, the values and principles which guide government policy must find expression as purposes from which specific aims and targets are subsequently derived.

Purposes and implementation

Having dealt with overarching values and principles, I turn now to matters of purpose and implementation. Here our initial questions concern the congruence between values and stated aims. Do publicly stated policy aims and targets cohere with expressed values or principles, or is there dissonance between the two? If published policy aims do not appear to coincide with a government's stated values and principles, can some hidden agenda, some unspoken aims, be discovered? What are the causes of the mismatch? Let us suppose, for example, that a government declares itself to support comprehensive civil rights for disabled people, but produces attenuated policy and legislation inadequate to fulfil that aim. Are we to conclude that the stated values and aims were not the true values and aims, or that the goals were not fully realisable when negotiated in the real world, or that external factors, by *force majeure*, have prevented government from pursuing its aims? How feasible is the realisation of an aim? Just how much progress towards an aim is reasonable? These are fine judgements that must be made in the knowledge of past experience, comparative examples and contemporary conditions. The main point of analysis here, however, is the extent of contiguity between values and purposes.

The movement from the theoretical to the practical brings us to the next part of the analytical process, which is concerned with implementation. Here we must discover the extent to which organisations and structures designed to implement policy are appropriate to the fulfilment of stated aims and targets (Page, 1985; Mouzelis, 1975). For example, a government may enact legislation to protect the civil rights of a certain group within the population. However, if the legal redress available is weak or ill-defined, and if a monitoring body such as a rights commission is underfunded and limited in scope, then doubt arises as to whether this structure for implementation can ensure that the stated aim (civil rights for a particular group) will be satisfactorily achieved. The further question is whether the mode of implementation was merely flawed or whether the government wished merely to *appear* to be extending civil rights while it was actually pursuing other aims such as, for example, protecting businesses against expensive legal action or additional costs.

Operation and practice

So far we have considered values, principles, purposes and implementation, but the delivery of policy is grounded in structures, operations and practices. Any analysis must therefore assess the performance of the organisations and staff whose job it is to realise policy. The key question here concerns the extent to which management and everyday practice support stated aims and targets. Certainly, employees may agree with policy wholeheartedly, but it is just as possible that they may oppose it with great vigour. In assessing the actual outcomes, therefore, we must be aware not only of the structure, but also the practice, of implementation. It may be, for example, that legislation was cogently framed and appropriate structures were put in place, only for the realisation of policy to be affected by the way in which the necessary work was actually done (Rollinson *et al.*, 1998; Burrell and Morgan, 1979; Jenkins, 1978). The thwarting of policy aims may arise either dramatically through concerted subversion or incompetence, or, more mundanely, by operational problems. (Burrell, 1999a,b; Brown, 1999; Nisse, 1998).

The final part of policy analysis concerns the results. Scholars researching new social policy face the problem that outcomes may still lie in the future. Sometimes they have to work with little more than early estimates, initial indications or even no data at all concerning a policy's effects. Where outcomes are available, an important question is the extent to which actual results concur with original goals and targets.

Even where outcomes do match initially stated aims we must be careful not to make the automatic assumption that the targets were met *because of* the policy. We must look for other (external) factors that may have produced the outcomes irrespective of the policy. If, on the other hand, outcomes did not match policy aims, the task is to discover why this mismatch came about. In sum, we must ask whether outcomes may accord more closely with other values and principles than those originally claimed. If there is a disjuncture between principles and outcomes, why is this?

Outcomes

Our evaluation of some particular policy or set of policies may reveal that outcomes do not coincide with stated principles, intentions and targets. There are at least five reasons why aims and outcomes may differ and why policies may 'fail'. These are:

1. inadequate policy formulation;
2. poor structural implementation;
3. poor (or even subversive) practice;
4. the intervention of unforeseen external circumstances; and
5. that the stated or overt aims were not the real intentions, instead, outcomes concur with covert aims.

(1) Inadequate or contested policy formulation. A government may have certain values and principles, and may articulate certain aims, but may fail to achieve these because the policy it formulates is inadequate. For example, a government may believe that certain ends can

be achieved by a policy of *voluntary* regulation whereas in reality those affected would only act if *compelled* to do so. Equally, a government may develop a policy to achieve certain aims but not make available the finance or other resources necessary to achieving such aims. Then again, there may be disruptive pressures arising, not from external environments, but from within governing parties themselves. We may recall the strife faced by the Conservatives under John Major on the question of Britain's role within the European Union. At one stage the differences of opinion became so intense that political pundits asked whether the party stood in danger of shattering into several factions (White, 1997; Young, 1996; Macaskill, 1996).

(2) Poor structural implementation. A government may construct an effective policy and provide the resources needed to carry it through. However, the organisational structure intended to enact a policy may be flawed or ineffective. For example, the Conservatives under John Major believed that absent parents should contribute to the upkeep of their children and so in 1993 set up the Child Support Agency (Alcock, 1996). In its early years, however, the agency was beset by significant problems, encountered substantial public criticism, and performed less well than had been expected (Brown and Schaefer, 1999; Grice, 1999).

(3) Poor practice or dissent. The governance of Britain is now shared between supranational (European), national (UK), national devolved (Scotland, Wales) and local administrations. It is not unusual for one political party to have a majority at one level, but for its opponents to be in control at another. Accordingly, a party at national level may desire to see a policy implemented locally, but meet with fierce resistance. So, for example, some socialist authorities mounted a particularly vigorous rearguard action against the sale of council houses under the (Conservative government's) 'Right to Buy' Act of 1980. In the end the government threatened to take central control over certain local authorities' functions in this matter (Walker, D., 1982).

(4) External circumstances. A government may wish to achieve certain ends and may build and implement a cogent policy backed by ample resources and still obtain poor outcomes, not as a result of any internal (political) shortcomings, but due to the disruptive impact of external circumstances. Every administration must cope with unlooked-for pressures and events that may at times reduce policy to little more than pragmatic reaction (Blakemore, 1998, chapter 5; Hill,

1998). In modern times phenomena such as global markets, new technology and the almost instantaneous transfer of information can have
unpredictable effects (Giddens, 1999; Midgley, 1997). Historically,
we may think of the impacts of war, the Great Depression of the
1930s, the oil crisis of the 1970s, and the turmoil in the Asian 'tiger'
economies during the late 1990s. All of these events had profound
effects on domestic economies and on social policy writ large. A further factor in the impact of policy may be public opposition. For
example, towards the end of 1999 the British government commis-
sioned large-scale research that could, ultimately, allow the commercial production and sale in Britain of genetically modified foods.
However, public sympathy appeared dead set against genetic modifi-
cation and the supermarkets insisted that their suppliers remove GM
ingredients from 'own brand' products (Hawkes and Nuttall, 1999;
Nuttall, 1999; Rhodes, 1999). It remains to be seen whose view prevails in the longer term.

(5) Covert policy aims. One other potential reason for a mismatch
between outcomes and stated aims may be that overt intentions are
not the true aims of policy, and that instead policy has been designed
to meet some other, covert ambitions. Taken all in all, then, we may
see that intentions and outcomes may fail to coincide for a number
of reasons. In these circumstances, an important task is to discover
reasons for incongruent or unexpected results.

Summary

Values, purposes, implementation and outcomes: the complexity of
interrelations between these components makes the evaluation of policy no easy task. Nor is there any guarantee that each of the four elements will tend to the same analytical conclusions. It may well be that
values and outcomes coincide *despite* practice, or that, notwithstanding genuine principles and aims, inadequate structures or inept practices may lead to wayward and unlooked-for outcomes. Again,
practitioners may be opposed to, and may thwart the principles at the
heart of a policy. Finally, external influences may lead to outcomes not
intended by either policy-makers or practitioners (Hill and Bramley,
1986). Notwithstanding these hazards and complexities, the task of
the policy analyst is to yield a subtle understanding of policy, and the
relations between values, purposes, implementation and outcomes.

Policy analysis: a worked example

Hitherto our appreciation of policy has been mainly in the abstract. To clarify the pertinence of the concepts at the heart of this book, I now offer a worked example of policy analysis. Several areas of welfare could have served our purposes here, but access to shelter is of particular importance in people's lives and political differences are thrown into particularly stark relief in British housing policy. Accordingly, I have chosen to review the 'Right to Buy' Acts of the 1980s, British legislation which transferred large quantities of state housing into private ownership. To set the broader context, I begin by using the political ideologies discussed in Chapter 2 to rehearse the spectrum of housing policy that different political beliefs could inform.

Political ideologies

(1) Fascist and racist policy. Historically, both fascist and racist policies have segregated groups of people according to some nominated criteria (race, colour, age, gender, disability). These groups have then encountered starkly differing responses from government. There might be equality for persons within a specific cohort, but people from different backgrounds would receive dissimilar treatment. Accordingly, under a fascist or racist regime, housing would be made available not on the basis of the need for shelter, but on some other factor such as skin colour, religious adherence or ethnic origin. Perhaps the most extreme forms of geographical segregation and differential treatment occurred in Nazi Germany, apartheid South Africa and, more recently, through 'ethnic cleansing' in the former Yugoslavia. However, away from these extreme instances, more diluted and covert forms of bias (racism, sexism, ageism, disablism) have been observed in modern democratic states. At this much less dramatic level, Smith (1996) has shown that during the 1960s, and irrespective of applicants' particular needs, a number of British local authorities allocated their better and more desirable housing stock to white families, and their poorer and less suitable housing to black and Asian families. Though it was not the official policy of these councils, discrimination took place as a matter of common practice. Smith also showed that some estate agents and mortgage companies exercised informal segregation by refusing to grant mortgages or

show properties in certain areas to potential buyers from ethnic minority communities.

(2) Neo-conservative or hard right policy. Those who believe in autonomous individualism or pure liberalism accept that each person enjoys equal status with others as a human being: each individual counts for one and no more than one. However, from a neo-liberal perspective the duty of the state may extend little further than ensuring fair contracts within a free market. What kinds of housing policy might such a government produce? Clearly, it would be loath to build and superintend state-owned housing and if some previous government had entered into housing provision a neo-conservative administration would seek to reduce and, perhaps, ultimately abolish the state's role as landlord. Housing would be privatised so that it became a commodity in the free market. We would also expect to see the deregulation of rents so that supply and demand would dictate the market price (rent) between landlords and tenants. Housing benefits, inasmuch as they distort market conditions, might be reduced or abolished. We would also expect to see the reduction of building and planning regulations, allowing individuals to decide what to build where. Perhaps the government's major residual role might be to ensure respect for, and the legal rights of, property ownership. (Minford, 1991; Green, 1990; Harris, R., 1988, 1987, 1980; Seldon, 1983; Acton and Seldon, 1961.)

(3) Moderate or 'one nation' conservative policy. A less 'pure' strand of conservatism might mitigate some market orientated policies through a sense of *noblesse oblige*. Here, 'one nation' Conservatives would accept an obligation to protect the weakest in society and policies would therefore temper an enthusiasm for the market with state intervention to provide residual services on the basis of need (Raison, 1990; Prior, 1986; Macmillan, 1978; Butler, 1971).

(4) Policies under social democracy/democratic socialism. As we move further to the left of the political spectrum we find even less willingness to rely on the market to solve accommodation problems and greater interest in state and collective solutions. Under social democracy, we might expect to see limits placed on the rent and conditions that landlords could impose on tenants. We would also find the state more active in providing housing at affordable rents for poorer families who could not afford to buy their own homes on the

open market (Balchin, 1995; Malpass and Murie, 1994; Arblaster and Hatwin, 1993; Forrest and Murie, 1988).

(5) Communist policy. Under hard left doctrines, little room would be left for markets. In a command economy in which assets were produced as directed by state planning, housing would be built, owned and supplied by the state. Assuming that the particular regime in charge was not corrupt, we would expect to seeing housing allocated according to the needs of families (Mathey, 1990; Sillince, 1990).

(6) Communitarian approaches. Communitarians argue for structural changes in the location and level of government itself. Moreover, communitarians contend that the variety of policy responses must recognise and respect the heterogeneity of social groups (Young, 1990; George and Wilding, 1985). From this perspective, society is a plural entity in which groups with different social, cultural and ethnic backgrounds have different needs and require different qualities of response from a multifaceted and multi-level state. Communitarian thinkers therefore concentrate on housing problems that arise from the 'universal' thinking of traditional political doctrines. These problems may include, for example, gender inequalities in access to housing where the norm in a society is that of the male breadwinner and female homemaker (Pahl, 1989); the problems encountered by extended families in finding suitable accommodation when the overwhelming provision of housing is for smaller nuclear families and people living alone (Balchin, 1995; Malpass and Murie, 1994), and the problems experienced by disabled people where general housing designs are ill-suited to their requirements (Imrie, 1996; Imrie and Wells, 1993; Barnes, 1991).

The 'Right to Buy' policy

Having reviewed a political spectrum of housing policy positions, I now move to the specific example of the 'Right to Buy' legislation of the 1980s. The policy was introduced by Margaret Thatcher early in her first administration and it involved the sale of council housing and flats principally to sitting tenants. We should bear in mind that our chief purpose here is to understand analysis rather than digress into a detailed discussion of housing policy per se. I have taken an older, instead of more recent, example because the passage of time allows us more clearly to observe the consequences of the policy. The main questions are, why was the policy introduced, how was it implemented, and what were the chief outcomes? The key elements of the analysis are (as before): values; purposes; implementation; practice, and outcomes.

Values and principles. The values that stood at the core of Margaret Thatcher's Conservative Party were those of individualism, independence, tradition, freedom of choice and free market economics (Thatcher, 1993; Minford, 1991; Green, 1990; Harris, D., 1988, 1987, 1980; Scruton, 1984; Seldon, 1983; Acton and Seldon, 1961). The party opposed socialism, and was generally antagonistic towards to state-organised, collective interventions in society. It also had a fondness for British custom and tradition. The values of independence and 'choice' informed the principles that guided the 'Right to Buy' policy, as explained by Margaret Thatcher (1993: 39) in her autobiography. She wrote that her government's programme was designed to 'reverse socialism, extend choice and widen property ownership'.

Purposes. The specific purposes or aims of the 'Right to Buy' policy were also made clear by Thatcher (1993: 39):

> We would give council tenants the right to buy their homes at large discounts, with the possibility of 100 per cent mortgages. There would be partial deregulation of new private sector renting. (Decades of restrictive controls had steadily reduced the opportunities for those who wished to rent accommodation and thereby retarded labour mobility and economic progress.)

Her government's purposes, then, were to reduce the state's role as landlord, to increase private ownership of property, and, by reducing the amount of regulation, to increase the amount of private sector rented accommodation available. Two further purposes were economic rather than environmental. First, the government wished to reduce overall public expenditure. The sell-off could diminish subsequent capital spending and could also yield a reduction in housing subsidies to local authorities. Second, it desired to increase the amount of private accommodation for rent as a way of helping the labour force to become more mobile. Minford *et al.* (1987) argued that unemployment could be reduced by 2 per cent if the housing market was freed from excessive control and regulation.

Implementation. The policy was first given effect through the Housing Act, 1980. With a few exceptions, the Act gave secure tenants the right to buy their council homes at substantial discounts (between 33 and 50 per cent) to the market price, depending on the number of years they had been secure tenants. The Act also gave secure tenants the right to a mortgage up to the full purchase price. The government anticipated that local authorities (especially those where opposition parties held control) might seek to foil its intentions. Section 23(3) of the Act therefore empowered the Secretary of State 'to do all such things as appear to him necessary or expedient to enable secure tenants ... to exercise the right to buy and the right to a mortgage'.

Practice. Practice varied according to the political sympathies of the local authority concerned. Some authorities were keen supporters of the right to buy, but others were dead set against it. Initially at least, these rather polarised positions produced a differential impact of the overall policy depending on the political complexion of the region involved. Labour-led councils like St Helens on Merseyside and Peterborough in the East were vehemently opposed to the sale of council houses, sharing the pressure group Shelter's view that the policy amounted to 'asset-stripping'. Norwich Council attempted to conserve its public housing stock by refusing or delaying sales. However, Michael Heseltine, then Environment Secretary, used his powers under the legislation to take over direct control of sales. Norwich subsequently lost a legal appeal against the move (Walker, D., 1982). The power of the central government meant that, at best, local opponents of the policy could do little more than cause delays to implementation.

Other councils, usually Conservative controlled, were by and large much more favourable to the policy and went ahead with sales with some alacrity. An extraordinary situation arose in Conservative-held Torbay. The council wished to divest itself of all its council housing. A ballot was held: 787 people declared in favour of privatisation, 2,210 voted against, but 2,209 abstained. Under the government's rules, abstentions were to be treated as a vote *in favour* of a sell-off. However, the then Minister of Housing, Nicholas Ridley, knew that a political storm would break around his ears should he allow the transfer go ahead on the flimsy pretext that the abstentions were really votes in favour. He therefore asked the council to re-run the ballot since 'the view of the tenants had not become clear' (Forrest and Murie, 1988).

Outcomes

> By the end of the third term of the Conservative government, well over one
> million local authority dwellings had been sold under the Right to Buy,
> new construction had virtually ceased and the transfer of council estates to
> other landlords had become a reality (Cole and Furbey, 1994: 180).

Of the several consequences that flowed from the 'Right to Buy' legislation, some were intended, but there were also a number of effects
that were unanticipated. The key outcomes I deal with here include
the sale of a large quantity of council stock, subsequent effects on
housing waiting lists and on homelessness, and impacts on house
builders (especially those who built starter homes).

(1) Impacts on local authorities. The common experience of local
authorities was that their best properties were bought by sitting tenants
while the poorer stock remained in council hands. Even within the
first four years it became clear that sales under the 'Right to Buy' legislation had led to a distinct reduction in the overall quality of council
housing (Forrest and Murie, 1984). However, they were not permitted
to keep and reinvest the proceeds of council house sales, either to
replace the losses or to upgrade the remaining dwellings. Instead, the
greater proportion of the revenue was clawed back by the Treasury to
offset other public expenditure so that in 1994 (for example) starts
were made on only 500 new local authority houses (Lund, 1996). As
their role diminished, what was envisaged for local authorities in the
future? The government argued that councils should become 'strategic
enablers'. This involved assessing housing needs in their local areas
and meeting such needs by facilitating the work of other housing
providers (Department of the Environment, 1987).

(2) The impact of sales on council housing stock. Between 1980 and
1994 the sale of houses exceeded 1.5 million. The peak years were
1982 (196,430 sales) and 1983 (138,511 sales). In 1988, following
further legislation to increase the discount available on council flats to
a maximum of 70 per cent, there was a fresh wave of buying: 160,568
in 1988 and 181,370 properties in 1989 (Wilcox, 1995). In 1979 local
authorities owned about 30 per cent of the housing stock. By 1995 the
proportion had declined to 22 per cent, (Lund, 1996) and by 1998
the proportion had declined to just 16 per cent (Department of the
Environment, 2000). The aim to reduce the state's role as a landlord
had been accomplished.

(3) Impacts on rented accommodation in the private sector. Deregulation of the private rented sector had been a common theme of post-war Conservative policy. For example, Harold Macmillan provided substantial deregulation through the Rent Act of 1957 (Timmins, 1996). However, despite Thatcher's attempts to stimulate growth in the private rented sector by further deregulation, the availability of this kind of accommodation did not increase. In 1979 some 12 per cent of the total dwelling stock was privately rented, but by 1993 the proportion had fallen to just 10 per cent. This particular policy goal was, therefore, not met. However, deregulation did have a number of outcomes that were, for tenants, unfortunate and undesirable.

The warnings from history were clear. Some landlords had taken the opportunity, after Macmillan's Rent Act of 1957, to make money by raising rents. Perhaps the most notorious example was that of Perec Rachman, who bought up short leases in big, multiple-occupation houses in west London. In order to re-let the properties at higher rents, he removed the sitting tenants using methods which Timmins (1996: 189) describes as 'never too gentle'. One member of Mrs Thatcher's cabinet, Peter Walker (Secretary of State for Energy from 1979 to 1983) had witnessed the exploitation of tenants when, in 1970, he was appointed Minister of Housing and Local Government by Ted Heath. Walker (1991: 139) recorded some of his early ministerial experiences:

One of my first actions had been to look at housing in Brixton. I remember going into one room which housed a West Indian family of a man, his wife and two children. It was without windows but immaculately clean, with Christian pictures and crucifixes on the walls. I expressed my horror and asked how much they paid in rent. When they told me, I pointed out that there was legislation to stop this kind of extortion. They said they had agreed to pay it and having done so it would be wrong to go and try to get it changed. Fortunately, this particular family were offered council accommodation shortly afterwards.

The policy of deregulation not only failed to stimulate more accommodation in the private sector, it also did nothing to halt the widespread neglect of properties. In 1991 some 20.5 per cent of privately rented stock was unfit for habitation, as opposed to 6.9 per cent of council housing and 6.7 per cent of housing association properties (Department of the Environment, 1991).

Table 8.1   Households accepted as
statutorily homeless, 1984–91 England

Year	Number of acceptances
1984	80,500
1985	91,010
1986	100,490
1987	109,170
1988	113,770
1989	122,180
1990	140,350
1991	144,780

Source: adapted from Burrows *et al., Homelessness
as Social Policy*, Routledge Ltd (1997: 13); and
Department of the Environment Information Bulletin,
1996, National Statistics. © Crown Copyright 2000

(4) Impacts on homelessness. Levels of homelessness and, more
especially, rooflessness, are notoriously difficult to calculate with
any real accuracy. Greve (1991) estimated that in the decade to 1990
over a million households (some 3 million people) were accepted by
local councils as homeless. The figure grew year after year as council
stock dwindled (Table 8.1).

Thatcher (1993) acknowledged the severity of the problem during
her premiership. Dealing with the period 1988–9 she wrote (p. 603):

> The most disturbing political issue in housing at this time, however, was
> homelessness. It should immediately be said that the alarmingly large fig-
> ures for the 'homeless' did not by definition reflect the number of people
> without roofs over their heads. Rather, the published 'homelessness' fig-
> ures described the number of people in statutorily determined 'priority
> groups' who were accepted for housing. In other words, far from being
> homeless they had homes provided by local councils. Sad as the cases of
> some of these people might be, the problem which worried the general
> public – and me too – was the growing number of people (especially
> young people) sleeping rough on the streets of London and other big
> cities, who were better described as 'roofless'.

But have we said all when we acknowledge that people counted as
homeless 'far from being homeless ... had homes provided by local
councils'? On the contrary, the figures were made up of those accepted
as homeless and in priority need under the relevant legislation,

and whom councils then had a duty *subsequently* to accommodate. Often, such accommodation took the form of temporary hostel arrangements or bed and breakfast places. The drying up of vacancies in public housing stock placed additional pressure on these kinds of emergency accommodation.

Thatcher did not attribute the problem of rooflessness either to the decrease in council housing occasioned by the 'Right to Buy' Act or to restrictions in board and lodging allowances (see below). Instead, while agreeing that there was a shortage of 'direct access' hostel accommodation, Thatcher (1993: 603) argued that the principal solution lay in the return of the young people back to their families. However, Andrews and Jacobs (1990) indicate that about 44 per cent of young people who used the Centrepoint Night Shelter in London in the late 1980s had been compelled to leave the family home as a result of suffering violence and abuse.

Burrows *et al.* (1997) nominate a number of factors, not mentioned by Thatcher, that rendered people vulnerable to homelessness. These included low income, lone parenthood (particularly where the children were at an age that meant they were dependent on the parent) and age (lone parents tended to be under 30). There is also some evidence that ethnicity played a part in vulnerability to homelessness (Greve *et al.*, 1971). As we have seen, homelessness increased, but assessing the numbers who were actually on the streets is far harder. There are clues to be found in the rise and fall of demand for places in night shelters and hostels. So, for example, following changes to board and lodging benefits in 1988, Centrepoint Night Shelter reported a 36 per cent increase in applications (Andrews and Jacobs, 1990). There is one final point here. Supporters of the 'Right to Buy' argued that the sale of council houses to their sitting tenants did not entail any diminution in the supply of housing, it simply changed the status of the occupants. How, therefore, could the policy be blamed for increased homelessness? The answer to this apparent contradiction is the reduction in turnover. Often, young couples rented council accommodation while they saved for the deposit to take out a mortgage to buy a home. But now many opted to buy their council house (at a discount price) instead and local authority housing stock therefore dwindled. The amount of properties becoming vacant in this way fell and waiting lists lengthened inexorably. With fewer houses, it became increasingly difficult for councils to meet even the demand from those declared to be in priority need. In passing, one might add that there were also, of course, consequences for the house building trade. During the 1980s,the demand for 'starter' homes collapsed as many secure tenants instead purchased their council homes under the 'Right to Buy'. Some councils were even left repaying subsidies on houses they no longer owned.

(5) Impacts on employment. Minford *et al.* (1987) had argued that Conservative policy should increase the mobility of the labour market and allow for a 2 per cent reduction in unemployment. Clearly, many factors other than housing policy will affect unemployment rates. Government economic policy, global economic trends and the performance of the domestic economy will have a far greater influence than housing measures. Nevertheless, it is appropriate to record that unemployment stood at 1,238,000 when Mrs Thatcher took office in May 1979, exceeding 2 million by November 1980 (Timmins, 1996), and peaking at 3.1 million in July 1986 (Government Statistical Service, 1994). The near trebling of unemployment therefore swamped any ameliorating effect that increased labour mobility may have bestowed.

Summary

The 'Right to Buy' policy accorded closely with neo-liberal values and purposes. Strong implementation resulted in the key aims, including the diminution of the role of the state as landlord, being achieved. In 1979 local authorities had provided about 30 per cent of the housing stock, by 1998 the proportion had been reduced to 16 per cent (Department of the Environment, 2000). While special needs housing (for older and disabled people) was exempted from compulsory sales, the 'Right to Buy' (compounded by changes to board and lodging allowances and housing benefits for young people aged under 18) yielded other undesirable and possibly unforeseen effects including large increases in homelessness, the exacerbation of councils' difficulties in aiding the homeless, and (through deregulation) a greater potential for the exploitation of vulnerable tenants in the private rental sector. Ultimately, the policy was successful in achieving what it set out to achieve; it was also popular and electorally advantageous. Indeed, so popular was it (politically speaking) that 'other main parties soon had to accommodate themselves to dropping their outright opposition' (Cole and Furbey, 1994: 180). At the same time, however, it made worse the position of certain groups of vulnerable people who could not command the resources necessary to secure a decent home.

We cannot be sure how far the policy would have been pressed. John Major's government seemed less dogmatic, and the advent of the New Labour government in May 1997 brought an altogether less doctrinaire approach to housing policy. In the event, therefore, local authorities still accounted for 16 per cent of domestic housing in June 2000 (Department of the Environment, 2000).

Finally, it is possible to draw from this analysis some conclusions about the (Thatcherite) Conservative view of citizenship. (It should be said that ordinarily one would wish to analyse not just one policy area but several, in order to make broader statements about overarching values and principles, but my purpose here is simply to illustrate a method of policy analysis.) For 'New Right' Conservatives *citizenship* is grounded in the autonomy and independence of the individual, which is itself secured through a command of resources, and, more especially, through the ownership of property (Beloff, 1984). In this vision of citizenship, the participation of the individual in society is based not on collective or mutual strategies, but on the competitive wielding of (social, economic and political) influence in order to shape society. The interference of the state in that competition is strictly curbed. The 'Right to Buy' enhanced the independence of many who came, for the first time, to own their own homes.

Almost inevitably, however, there were losers. Those unable to take advantage of the 'Right to Buy', even with the generous discounts on offer, were progressively trapped in (by and large) poorer council accommodation within distinct geographical locations. This process of segregation became known as 'social polarisation' (Malpass and Murie, 1994; Forrest and Murie, 1988). There was clear damage, therefore, to the quality of citizenship for those who became, and remained, homeless as a result of the policy, for those whose homes were subsequently repossessed by mortgage companies when they could not keep up payments, and for those whose homes and estates fell into increasing disrepair as council maintenance budgets were squeezed. The 'Right to Buy' policy was a blessing for some and a curse for others.

Conclusions

In this chapter I have outlined a pathway that leads from values, via policy implementation, to outcomes. I have shown how this route can provide a framework for policy analysis. Where governments have large majorities in Parliament, strong support in the country, and a fair wind in terms of the political climate, they may plan and implement policy substantially in accord with their values and aims. However, where governments are weak, or events conspire against them, they may enunciate policy principles but, for diverse reasons, be unable to invoke them. We have seen that external pressures, domestic circumstances, and internal administrative structures and practices can impinge on a government's capacity to govern.

External (world) factors may include treaty commitments and obligations, as well as the constraints arising from supranational bodies such as the United Nations or the European Union. There may also be other global circumstances at play including, for example, the economic and social impacts of climate change, major changes in economic trends or, even more dramatically, the impacts of war. Domestic circumstances can also affect a government's ability to abide by desired principles. These include political upheaval, economic difficulties and public resistence. Democratic governments tend to be acutely sensitive to the popularity of proposed policies. They may (notwithstanding declared principles) be forced to temper or even abandon their proposals in the face of large-scale public antagonism.

We have seen, then, that the pathway from values to results may be straightforward and direct, or convoluted and uncertain. Internal conflict between various sources of power, and the vagaries of external influences can make it difficult for an observer to establish the true intentions of government, and therefore difficult to measure outcomes against initial objectives. Even so, when we trace carefully the history of a policy from initiation to results it should be possible to make some sensible judgements about the congruence between a government's words and deeds, and if a policy is knocked off course by some external factors, these should be so significant as to be visible to the diligent policy analyst. In the final chapter I apply these ideas of analysis and evaluation to make several concluding observations about the place of British social policy in the modern European and global contexts.

9

Conclusions

This book has been concerned with the values and principles that stand behind social policies in Western democracies. The definition of terms like justice, liberty and equality is not straightforward. Meanings change over time and place. The extent of a government's political dogmatism and its understandings of these and similar values have profound consequences for the contours of the policies it creates. Equally, policy formulation takes place in the real world and many internal and external circumstances can disrupt a government's aims and objectives. The analysis of policy from values, through implementation, to outcomes is rendered all the more complex by having to take account of any disruptive influences and events.

In this ninth and final chapter, my aim is to consider social policy in the context of restructuring and change. The creation and implementation of social policy takes place within political structures which are themselves changing. The nation state is being challenged externally by globalisation, and internally by devolution. The autonomy of the nation state is under attack from above and below: from above in the increasing influence of the global economy and the proliferation of supranational bodies, and from below in increasing demands for devolution and self-government made by racially and culturally diverse groups. As the political landscape is refashioned, there will be consequences for the purpose and impact of social policy. Accordingly, the chapter ends with an assessment of possible futures for welfare in the twenty-first century.

Policy and changing political structures

Throughout the book, my consideration of social policy has been closely tied to the concept of the nation state. It would be wrong to draw to a close without recognising the profound changes that are now affecting Western democracies. I have argued that the existence and purpose of social policy is determined by principles derived from values prevailing in the governance of a state. But increasingly the questions are being put: what is a state, and what future is there for nation states as we have known them? Hall and Ikenberry (1989: 1–2) propose that a state comprises three elements:

> First, the state is a set of institutions; these are manned by the state's own personnel ... Second, these institutions are at the centre of a geographically bounded territory, usually referred to as a society ... Third, the state monopolises rule making within its territory. This tends towards the creation of a common political culture shared by all citizens.

In a highly uniform, centralised and autocratic state there may be only one set of values in the ascendant. Such a state may be 'absolutist', that is to say, it may be governed by some supreme and absolute authority (Vincent, 1987). The values dominant in such a state are likely, therefore, to promote the interests of one (ruling) portion of the population while subordinating the interests of others. It is equally likely that this imbalance may be reflected in the subsequent creation and application of policy. Alternatively, we may imagine a plural or devolved state in which a number of value systems may coexist. Here there will be limitations on the control that can be exercised over the lives of individuals (Young, 1990). These limitations will be expressed within a constitution that not only accepts diverse theories of knowledge but also allows for different perspectives in the creation of structures and the implementation of policies (Vincent, 1987). In this kind of 'pluralist' state there may be some key central principles that not only allow for, but also protect, diversity. These key principles will be 'plural' insofar as they acknowledge that within a given society there exist various groups holding to diverse values and norms which in turn lead to differing social and cultural desiderata. According to Vincent (p. 183):

> Political pluralism is a theory which views social life in terms of groups. The primary social entities are groups and they are not created by or even ultimately reliant upon any central authority ... The individual's primary allegiance is not to any abstract government but rather to groups, whether they be trade unions, churches, or local clubs. In consequence

they deny the absolute necessity of a highly unified legal or political order.

Clearly, then, 'plural' principles will allow for local influences over policy development and implementation. But, more crucially, the prime role of pluralistic principles is to secure equal respect ('fair play') for varying value systems and allow for the development of policies able to cope with the differential needs and wants of diverse groups in a population. The supporters of equality of opportunity argue that fair play is to be secured only where members of different groups can aspire under equal circumstances to positions of influence and authority within a state or within some particular substructure or institution of a state.

At the same time, however, we must recognise that there comes a point at which the notion of a state comes under so great a burden that it is difficult to speak of there being a state at all. In several European countries sub-national groups are agitating for greater autonomy (Roche, 1992). Prime examples include the Basques in Spain, the Walloons in Belgium, the fragmentation of the Soviet Union into its constituent republics, and the break-up of the former Yugoslavia along ethnic lines. We should remember that nation states no longer exercise autonomous government (if they ever did). International influences, the internet and global communications, the mobility of populations, the creation of supranational banks and stock exchanges, the growth of cross-boundary markets within a world economy, all these affect the ability of individual governments to pursue the policy aims they desire whether these be political, social or economic (Giddens, 1999).

The evidence suggests that government as an activity is becoming, at one and the same time, more diffuse and more centralised. As I write, government structures in Britain are being devolved to assemblies in Scotland, Wales and Northern Ireland (Bogdanor, 1999). The intention is to facilitate decision-making at more local levels. However, these assemblies will be subject to (and perhaps even more vulnerable to) the powerful forces of global finance and commerce, supranational political structures, including the European Union, and in addition they are likely to feel the uncertain economic effects of a single European currency.

The growing significance of both devolved and supranational political structures renders the task of policy analysis even more complicated than it already is. In assessing policy creation it becomes far more difficult to weigh the relative importance of sub-national, national and international forces. For example, public spending levels are subject not only to national economic conditions, but also (and increasingly) to the global market. Likewise, parochial policy-making may be influenced as much by external as by local considerations.

The movement of power away from the nation state, particularly towards supranational and global levels, may entail major consequences for the notion of citizenship (Turner, 1993). The danger of a weakened state is the attenuation of citizenship. How well can a weak government protect its citizens, either from outside forces or from each other? At the extreme, if a state can withstand neither international duress nor internal anarchy, of what value is it to be a citizen of that state? On the other hand, supranational treaties and accords may enhance rather than diminish citizenship. Protection under the constitution of a nation state may be strengthened by further rights derived from international agreements and supranational courts. For example, through the Human Rights Act 1998, Britain integrated into domestic law the European Convention on Human Rights (implementation of the Act took place in October 2000).

In sum, then, authority may be ceded 'upwards' to global forces and international bodies or 'downwards' to diverse sub-groups within a population. Such dispersal may go so far as to contravene Hall and Ikenberry's (1989) third element necessary for the definition of a state. If global and supranational forces become crucially influential, and if regional groups assert their own cultures and inaugurate their own constitutions, authorities and legal and civil structures, then the state no longer monopolises rule-making powers, nor (necessarily) do all citizens share a common political compact. The indications are that a flow of power away from nation states is, in fact, highly visible on the contemporary political scene and this has led Giddens (1999: 5) to contend that though they are still powerful, nation states are:

> being reshaped before our eyes. National economic policy can't be as effective as it once was. More importantly, nations have to rethink their identities now the older forms of geopolitics are becoming obsolete ... following the dissolving of the cold war, nations no longer have enemies. Who are the enemies of Britain, or France, or Japan? Nations today face risks and dangers rather than enemies, a massive shift in their very nature.
>
> Everywhere we look, we see institutions that appear the same as they used to be from the outside, and carry the same names, but inside have become quite different. We continue to talk of the nation, the family, work,

tradition, nature, as if they were all the same as in the past. They are not. The outer shell remains, but inside all is different – and this is happening not only in the US, Britain, or France, but almost everywhere.

Roche (1992) contends that citizenship, and especially the place of social rights within citizenship, will be greatly affected by the challenge to national sovereignty posed from above (at the global and European levels) and below by the internal autonomy sought by diverse ethnic and cultural groups. For Roche, the traditional notion that social rights were met through state welfare in response to national industry and commerce is now challenged on a number of fronts. I have mentioned the protraction of political authority from the national towards both the global and the local. But Roche also highlights changes in the structure of work towards high technology. There are new potential dangers stemming from nuclear power, genetic technology, and possible exhaustion of supplies (for example in food, the depletion of fish stocks in certain areas) which summon new social rights and duties into being. Roche argues that these new rights are political (extending beyond the boundaries of the nation state to the global level), ecological (protection of the environment as well as the individual), and temporal (in our current use of resources, consideration of our obligations to future generations).

Conclusion: between the global and the local – what future for policy?

The future of social policy as a child of the nation state will depend on several factors. Some indications are already available to us. First, since the early 1980s many Western European governments (including Sweden, Germany and Britain) have overseen a retrenchment in public spending, curtailment of public services, and some privatisation of welfare. Second, and perhaps as a consequence, there has been increasing inequality of wealth, the rich getting richer, the poor, poorer (Institute for Fiscal Studies, 1994). The upshot has been concern about the quality of citizenship enjoyed by the poorest in society, groups which may have become, in essence, disconnected from the community, and which some have labelled an 'underclass'. Many scholars argue that such exclusion is caused by the growth of economic inequalities (Mann, 1994; Brown, 1990). For others, the emergence of a 'deviant' culture has been caused, not by privatisation of welfare, but by the encouragement of dependence on the state in the first place (Green, 1990; Murray, 1990). Third, parties of the left and centre-left appear to have abandoned socialist and collective values in favour of a mixture of private and public approaches to welfare. In Britain this combination has been called the 'Third Way' (Giddens, 1998). A potential casualty of this composite approach is the concept of universal provision. In particular, the increasing longevity of older people has placed universal state pensions under particular pressure. Governments have been tempted more and more by managerialism, by privatised welfare and the use of means-testing (Clarke *et al.*, 1994; Wistow *et al.*, 1994; Farnham and Horton, 1992). All these indicators taken together suggest a more residual role for state welfare. However, depending on the particular patterns of devolution that transpire, the particular contours of any particular welfare system may, in future, be shaped as much at the local as at the national and supranational levels of government.

Postscript

Though my main purpose has been to analyse the connections between values, policies and outcomes, ultimately an individual's political judgements will be based on the beliefs to which he or she subscribes. Against the possibility that my prejudices have coloured the arguments in the book, I acknowledge a duty to declare my own particular values. I believe that principles and policies which approach the absolutes (either of unconstrained individual freedom or of compulsory mass equality) provide an inferior quality of citizenship than do those that regulate both liberty and choice within a framework of justice and equality of opportunity. Moreover, justice should concern itself with outcomes as much as with processes.

For many of those individuals who are gifted with inherited wealth, personal strength and high intelligence, the argument that governments should do no more than ensure fairness in the conduct of interaction and exchange, without regard to the inequalities that might arise, may be a convenient and persuasive one. However, greed is an ignoble, inelegant and, in the end, destructive guiding principle, not only for societies but for individuals as well. It may be true that many of the great advances in civilization have been linked neither to committees nor to the actions of the public in general, but to the names of individuals: Aristotle; Einstein; Shakespeare; Milton; Bach; Mozart;

Da Vinci; Galileo. But we should give due weight to the supportive environments within which people work and to the antecedents on which, at least in part, they depend. Perhaps it is wise to bear in mind the words of Sir Isaac Newton set down in a letter to his friend Robert Hooke: 'If I have seen further it is by standing on the shoulders of giants'. In the contemporary world, more and more advances result from the work of *teams* of researchers supported by public and commercial institutions. It is through the milieu of society that individuals make their contribution. Accordingly, the rights and duties of citizenship depend on the achievement of a balance between individual liberty and social responsibility.

Nor need we fear that to subscribe to equality of opportunity is to relinquish liberty. On the contrary, it is only through the fair conduct of civil life that freedom is to be discovered and enjoyed. For me, policies based on plural principles, those which respect equality of opportunity and support heterogeneity, offer the best comprise between freedom and equality. As to the dilemmas that scarce resources may bring, even using plural principles it is not always possible or desirable coldly to measure one heartbreaking need against another. It is not always true that there is a 'right' decision. It is not always clear, even with hindsight, whether a particular policy was 'right' or 'wrong'. In any event, human beings will always make mistakes: how else are we to learn?

Bibliography

Abbasi, K. (1998) 'Is medical school selection discriminatory?', *British Medical Journal*, **317**: 1097–8.

Abberley, P. (1987) 'The concept of oppression and the development of a social theory of disability', *Disability, Handicap and Society*, **2**(1): 5–19.

Abberley, P. (1996) 'Work, Utopia and Impairment' in Barton, L. (ed.) *Disability and Society: Emerging Issues and Insights* (London: Longman).

Acton, H. B. and Seldon, A. (1961) *Agenda for a Free Society: Essays on Hayek's 'The Constitution of Liberty'* (London: Published for the Institute of Economic Affairs by Hutchinson).

Age Concern (1999a) *Pensioners Refused NHS Treatment New Survey Reveals* (London: Age Concern England).

Age Concern (1999b) *Older People and Discrimination in the NHS* (London: Age Concern England).

Ahmad, B. (1992) *Black Perspectives in Social Work* (Birmingham: Venture Press).

Alcock, P. (1993) *Understanding Poverty* (London: Macmillan).

Alcock, P. (1996) *Social Policy in Britain* (London: Macmillan).

Alcock, P., Erskine, A. and May, M. (1998) *The Student's Companion to Social Policy* (Oxford: Basil Blackwell).

Ali, Y. (1991) *Race and Citizenship* (London: Charter' 88).

Anderson, B. (1990) *Contracts and the Contract Culture* (London: Age Concern England).

Andrews, G. (ed.) (1991) *Citizenship* (London: Lawrence & Wishart).

Andrews, K. and Jacobs, J. (1990) *Punishing the Poor: Poverty under Thatcher* (London: Macmillan).

Apthorpe, R. (1979) *Public Policy Evaluation* (The Hague: Institute of Social Studies).

Arblaster, L. and Hawtin, M.(1993) *Health, Housing and Social Policy: Homes for Wealth or Health*? (London: Socialist Health Association).

Arendt, H. (1968) 'What is Freedom?' in Arendt H., *Between Past and Future* (New York: Viking).

Arnstein, S. (1969) 'A ladder of citizen participation', *American Institute of Planners Journal*, **35**(4): 216–24.

Atkinson, A. B. (1983) *Social Justice and Public Policy* (London: Harvester Wheatsheaf).

Bachrach, P. and Baratz, M. S. (1970) *Power and Poverty: Theory and Practice* (London: Oxford University Press).

Baker, J. (1987) *Arguing for Equality* (London: Verso).

Balchin, P. (1995) *Housing Policy* (London: Routledge).

Baldock, J., Manning, N., Miller, S. and Vickerstaff, S. (eds) (1999) *Social Policy* (Oxford: Oxford University Press).

Baldwin, A. (1975) 'Mass removals and separate development', *Journal of Southern African Studies*, **1**: 215–27.

Barbalet, J. M. (1993) 'Citizenship, Class Inequality and Resentment' in Turner, B. S. (ed.) *Citizenship and Social Theory* (London: Sage).

Barker, I. and Peck, E. (eds) (1987) *Power in Strange Places: User Empowerment in Mental Health Services* (London: Good Practices in Mental Health).

Barnes, C. (1991) *Disabled People in Britain and Discrimination: A Case for Anti-discrimination Legislation* (London: Hurst).

Barnes, C. and Oliver, M. (1998) *Disabled People and Social Policy: From Exclusion to Inclusion* (London: Longman).

Barnes, C., Mercer, G. and Shakespeare, T. (1999) *Exploring Disability: A Sociological Introduction* (Cambridge: Polity Press).

Barret, M. and Phillips, A. (1992) *Destabilizing Theory* (Cambridge: Polity Press).

Barry, B. (1965) *Political Argument* (London: Routledge & Kegan Paul).

Barry, N. (1990) 'Markets, Citizenship and the Welfare State: Some Critical Reflections, in Plant, R. *Citizenship and Rights in Thatcher's Britain* (London: Institute of Economic Affairs Health and Welfare Unit).

Barton, L. (1986) 'The politics of special educational needs', *Disability, Handicap and Society*, **1**(3): 273–90.

Bassnett, S. (1999) 'View from here', *The Independent, Education Supplement*, 8 April: 2.

Behrens, R. (1993) 'Managing diversity', *Viewpoint: The Magazine for Benefit Agency Managers* (Summer), **8**: 19.

Behrens, R. and Auluck, R. (1993) *Action Planning for Diversity Management: A Comparative Perspective* (London: Southern Africa Development Unit, United Kingdom Civil Service).

Beinart, W. and DuBow, S. (eds) (1995) *Segregation and Apartheid in Twentieth Century South Africa* (London: Routledge).

Beloff, M. (1984) *Freedom and Property* (London: Conservative Political Centre).

Bentham, J. (1776) *Fragment on Government* [1988 edition: J. H. Burns and H. L. A. Hart (eds)] (Cambridge: Cambridge University Press).

Bentham, J. (1780) *Introduction to Principles and Morals of Legislation* [1996 edition: J. H. Burns and H. L. A. Hart (eds)] (Oxford: Oxford University Press).

Berer, M. (1988) 'Whatever happened to "a woman's right to choose"?', *Feminist Review*, **29**: 24–37.

Beresford, P. and Croft, S. (1984) 'Welfare pluralism: the new face of Fabianism?, *Critical Social Policy*, **9**: 19–39.

Beresford, P. and Croft, S. (1989) 'User involvement, citizenship and social policy, *Critical Social Policy*, **26**: 5–18.

Beresford, P. and Croft, S. (1993) *Citizen Involvement* (London: Macmillan).

Berger, P. and Luckmann, T. (1967) *The Social Construction of Reality* (London: Allen Lane & Penguin).

Berlin, I. (1969a) *Four Essays on Liberty* (Oxford: Oxford University Press).

Berlin, I. (1969b) 'Equality' in Blackstone, W. T. (ed.) *The Concept of Equality* (Minneapolis: Burgess).

Berthoud, R., Lakey, J. and McKay, S. (1993) *The Economic Problems of Disabled People* (London: Policy Studies Institute).

Bevan, A. (1952) *In Place of Fear* (London: Heinemann).

Beveridge, Sir W. (1942) *Social Insurance and Allied Services*, Cmd 6404 (London: HMSO).

Blackaby, D., Clark, K., Drinkwater, S., Leslie, D., Murphy, P. and O'Leary, N. (1998) *Earnings and Employment Opportunities for People with Disabilities: Secondary Analysis using the Census, General Household Survey and the Labour Force Survey* (Swansea: University of Wales Swansea).

Blackstone, W. T. (ed.) (1969) *The Concept of Equality* (Minneapolis: Burgess).

Blackstone, W. T. (1973) *Political Philosophy: An Introduction* (New York: Thomas Y. Crowell).

Blair, T. (1998) *The Third Way: New Politics for the New Century* (London: Fabian Society).

Blair, T. (1995) Let *Us Face the Future – the 1945 Anniversary* Lecture (London: Fabian Society).

Blakemore, K. (1998) *Social Policy* (Buckingham: Open University Press).

Blakemore, K. and Boneham, M. (1994) *Age, Race and Ethnicity: A Comparative Approach* (Buckingham: Open University Press).

Blakemore, K. and Drake, R.F. (1996) *Understanding Equal Opportunity Policies* (London: Prentice Hall/Harvester Wheatsheaf).

Blom Cooper, L. (1985) *A Child in Trust: The Report of the Panel of Inquiry into the Circumstances Surrounding the Death of Jasmine Beckford* (Wembley: London Borough of Brent).

Bobrow, D. B. and Dryzek, J. S. (1987) *Policy Analysis by Design* (Pittsburgh: University of Pittsburgh Press).

Bock, G. and James, S. (eds) (1992) *Beyond Equality and Difference: Citizenship, Feminist Politics and Female Subjectivity* (London: Routledge).

Bogdanor, V. (1979) *Devolution* (Oxford: Oxford University Press).

Bogdanor, V. (1999) *Devolution in the United Kingdom* (Oxford: Oxford University Press).

Boucher, D. and Kelly, P. (1994) *The Social Contract from Hobbes to Rawls* (London: Routledge).

Boudon, R. (1974) *Education, Opportunity, and Social Inequality: Changing Prospects in Western Society* (London: Wiley-Interscience).

Bowie, N. (ed.) (1988) *Equal Opportunity* (Boulder: Westview Press).

Bradshaw, J. and Holmes, H. (1989) *Living on the Edge: A Study of the Living Standards of Families on Benefit in Tyne and Wear* (Newcastle: Tyneside Child Poverty Action Group).

Bramley, G., Bartlett, W. and Lambert, C. (1995) *Planning, the Market and Private Housebuilding* (London: UCL Press).

Brown, C. (1999) 'Straw offers £10 passport sweetener', *The Independent*, 1 July: 5.

Brown, C. and Schaefer, S. (1999) 'Lying to the CSA to be criminalised' *The Independent*, 19 June: 2.

Brown, H. P. (1988) *Egalitarianism and the Generation of Inequality* (Oxford: Clarendon Press).

Brown, J. (1990) *Victims or Villains? Social Security Benefits in Unemployment* (York: Joseph Rowntree Memorial Trust).

Bulmer, M. and Solomos, J. (eds) (1999) *Racism* (London: Routledge).

Bulmer, M., Lewis, J. and Piachaud, D. (1989) *The Goals of Social Policy* (London: Unwin).

Burrell, G. and Morgan, G. (1979) *Sociological Paradigms and Organisational Analysis: Elements of the Sociology of Corporate Life* (London: Heinemann Educational).

Burrell, I. (1999a) 'Passport crisis "known about for months" ', *The Independent,* 7 July: 8.

Burrell, I. (1999b) 'Straw climbdown on passport chaos', *The Independent,* 2 July: 7.

Burrows, R. and Loader, B. (1994) *Towards a Post-Fordist Welfare State* (London: Routledge).

Burrows, R., Gilbert, N. and Pollert, A. (1992) 'Fordism, Post-Fordism and Economic Flexibility' in Gilbert, N., Burrows, R. and Pollert, A. (eds) *Fordism, Flexibility and Change* (London: Macmillan).

Burrows, R., Pleace, N. and Quilgars, D. (eds) (1997) *Homelessness and Social Policy* (London: Routledge).

Butler, R. A. (1971) *The Art of the Possible: The Memoirs of Lord Butler, K.G., C.H.* (London: Hamilton).

Cahill, M. (1999) 'The Environment and Green Social Policy' in Baldock, J., Manning, N., Miller, S. and Vickerstaff, S. (eds) *Social Policy* (Oxford: Oxford University Press).

Calvert, P.(1983) *Politics, Power and Revolution: An Introduction to Comparative Politics* (Brighton: Harvester Wheatsheaf).

Campbell, J. and Oliver, M. (1996) *Disability Politics: Understanding Our Past, Changing Our Future* (London: Routledge).

Carsten, F. L. (1976) 'Interpretations of Fascism' in Laqueur, W. (ed.) *Fascism: A Reader's Guide* (Aldershot: Wildwood House).

Central Statistical Office (1996) *Social Trends* (London: HMSO).

Charles, N. (2000) *Feminism, the State and Social Policy* (London: Macmillan).

Clare, J. (1999) 'Women graduates earn less than men', *Daily Telegraph,* 17 April: 17.

Clark, A. and Hirst, M. (1989) 'Disability in adulthood: ten year follow up of young people with disabilities', *Disability, Handicap and Society,* **4**: 271–83.

Clarke, J., Cochrane, A. and McLaughlin, E. (eds) (1994) *Managing Social Policy* (London: Sage).

Clasen, J. (1999) *Comparative Social Policy, Concepts, Theories and Methods* (Oxford: Basil Blackwell).

Cloward, R. and Ohlin, L. (1960) *Delinquency and Opportunity* (New York: Free Press).

Cochrane, A. and Clarke, J. (1993) *Comparing Welfare States* (London: Sage).

Cohan, A. S. (1975) *Theories of Revolution: An Introduction* (London: Nelson).

Cohen, A. (1955) *Delinquent Boys* (New York: Free Press).

Cohen, S. (1985) *Visions of Social Control* (Cambridge: Polity Press).

Cole, I. and Furbey, R. (1994) *The Eclipse of Council Housing* (London: Routledge).

Cole, M. (1989) *Educating for Equality: Some Guidelines for Good Practice* (London: Routledge).

Colebatch, H. K. (1998) *Policy* (Buckingham: Open University Press).

Commission on Social Justice (1994) *Social Justice: Strategies for National Renewal*; *The Report of the Commission on Social Justice* (London: Vantage).

Cosin, B., Flude, M. and Hales, M. (1989) School, *Work and Equality: A Reader* (London: Hodder & Stoughton).

Cowling, M. (1963) *Mill and Liberalism* (Cambridge: Cambridge University Press).

Craib, I. (1992) *Modern Social Theory* (London: Harvester Wheatsheaf).

Cranston, M. (1967) *Freedom, A New Analysis* (London: Longman).

Crenson, M. (1971) *The Un-Politics of Air Pollution* (Baltimore: Johns Hopkins Press).

Crick, B. (1984) *Socialist Values and Time* (London: Fabian Society).

Crick, B. (1992) 'Well, is equality dead?' in Newton, M. and Hall, S. *Is Equality Dead?* (London: Fabian Society).

Croft, S. and Beresford, P. (1989) 'User involvement, citizenship and social policy', *Critical Social Policy*, **26**: 5–18.

Dahl, R. (1957) 'The Concept of Power', *Behavioural Science*, **2**: 201–5.

Dahl, R. (1961) *Who Governs?* (New Haven: Yale University Press).

Dahrendorf, R. (1969) 'On the Origin of Social Inequality' in Blackstone, W. T. (ed.) *The Concept of Equality* (Minneapolis: Burgess).

Dahrendorf, R. (1975) *The New Liberty, Survival and Justice in a Changing World* (London: Routledge & Kegan Paul).

Dahrendorf, R. (1987) 'The erosion of citizenship and its consequences for us all', *New Statesman and Society*, 12 June.

Davis, A. (1996) 'Women and the Personal Social Services' in Hallett, C. (ed.) *Women and Social Policy: An Introduction* (Hemel Hempstead: Prentice Hall/Harvester Wheatsheaf).

Dean, H. and Taylor Gooby, P. (1992) *Dependency Culture* (Hemel Hempstead: Harvester Wheatsheaf).

Demaine, J. and Entwistle, H. (1996) *Beyond Communitarianism: Citizenship, Politics and Education* (London: Macmillan).

Department of Health and Social Security (1974) *Report of the Committee of Inquiry into the Care and Supervision provided by Local Authorities and Other Agencies in Relation to Maria Colwell and the Co-ordination Between Them* (London: HMSO).

Department of the Environment (1987) *Housing: The Government's Proposals*, Cm 214 (London: HMSO).

Department of the Environment (1991) *English House Condition Survey* (London: HMSO).

Department of the Environment (2000) *Housing: Key Figures – June 2000* (London: Department of the Environment). [www.open.gov.uk]

Digby, A. (1989) *British Welfare Policy: Workhouse to Workfare* (London: Faber & Faber).

Downing, D. and Bazargan, S. (1991) *Image and Ideology in Modern/Postmodern Discourse* (Albany: University of New York Press).

Doyal, L. and Gough, I. (1990) *A Theory of Human Need* (London: Macmillan).

Drabble, M. (1988) *Case for Equality* (London: Fabian Society).

Drake, R. F. (1992) 'Consumer participation, the voluntary sector and the concept of power', *Disability, Handicap and Society*, **7**(3): 301–12.

Drake, R. F. (1994) 'The exclusion of disabled people from positions of power in British voluntary organisations', *Disability and Society*, **9**(4): 461–80.

Drake, R. F. (1996a) 'A Critique of the Role of the Traditional Charities' in Barton, L. (ed.) *Disability and Society: Emerging Issues and Insights* (London: Longman).

Drake, R. F. (1996b) 'Charities, authority and disabled people: a qualitative study', *Disability and Society*, **11**(1): 5–23.

Drake, R. F. (1998) 'Housing and Older People' in Symonds, A. and Kelly, A. (eds) *The Social Construction of Community Care* (London: Macmillan).

Drake, R. F. (1999) *Understanding Disability Policies* (London: Macmillan).

Dummett, A. and Nicol, A. (1990) *Subjects, Citizens, Aliens and others*: *Nationality and Immigration Law* (London: Weidenfeld & Nicolson).

Dunn, J. (1980) *Political Obligation in its Historical Context: Essays in Political Theory* (Cambridge: Cambridge University Press).

Dunning, J. H. (1993) *Globalisation: The Challenge for National Economic Regimes* (Dublin: Economic and Social Research Institute) [Geary lectures; 24].

Dworkin, R. (1977) *Taking Rights Seriously* (London: Duckworth).

Dye, T. R. (1987) *Understanding Public Policy* (Englewood Cliffs: Prentice Hall).

Easton, D. (1965) A *Systems Analysis of Political Life* (New York: Wiley).

East Sussex County Council (1975) *Children at Risk*: A *Study by the East Sussex County Council into the Problems Revealed by the Report of the Inquiry into the Case of Maria Colwell* (Lewes: East Sussex County Council).

Eatwell, R. (1995) *Fascism, A History* (London: Chatto & Windus).

Edholm, F. (1991) 'The Unnatural Family' in Loney, M., Bocock, R., Clarke, J. *et al.* (eds) *The State or the Market: Politics and Welfare in Contemporary Britain* (London: Sage).

Edwards, J. (1987) *Positive Discrimination, Social Justice and Social Policy* (London: Tavistock).

Ehman, R. (1991) 'Rawls and Nozick: Justice Without Well-being' in Angelo Corlett, J. (ed.) *Equality and Liberty*: *Analyzing Rawls and Nozick* (London: Macmillan).

Einhorn, B., Kaldor, M. and Kavan, Z. (eds) (1996) *Citizenship and Democratic Control in Contemporary Europe* (Cheltenham: Edward Elgar).

Eisenstein, Z. (1989) *The Female Body and the Law* (Berkeley: University of California). *Encyclopaedia Britannica* (1997) 'South Africa', *Encyclopaedia Britannica*, (Chicago: Encyclopaedia Britannica Inc.)

Equal Opportunities Commission (1998a) *Briefing on Women and Men in Britain, 1997: 1. Pay* (Manchester: Equal Opportunities Commission).

Equal Opportunities Commission (1998b) *Briefing on Women and Men in Britain, 1997: 2. Education and Vocational Training in England and Wales* (Manchester: Equal Opportunities Commission).

Equal Opportunities Commission (1998c) *Briefing on Women and Men in Britain, 1997: 3. Work and Parenting* (Manchester: Equal Opportunities Commission).

Equal Opportunities Commission (1998d) *Briefing on Women and Men in Britain, 1997: 4. Income and Finance* (Manchester: Equal Opportunities Commission).

Esmail, A. (1997) 'Tackling racism in the NHS: we need action not words', *British Medical Journal*, 1 March, **314**: 618–19.

Esmail, A. and Everington, S. (1993) 'Racial discrimination against doctors from ethnic minorities', *British Medical Journal*, **306**: 691–2.

Esmail, A. and Everington, S. (1997) 'Asian doctors are still being discriminated against, *British Medical Journal*, 31 May, **314**: 1619.

Esmail, A., Everington, S. and Doyle, H. (1998) 'Racial discrimination in the allocation of distinction awards? Analysis of list of award holders by type of award, speciality and region', *British Medical Journal*, 17 January, **316**: 193–5.

Esmail, A., Nelson, P., Primarolo, D. and Toma, T. (1995) 'Acceptance into medical school and racial discrimination', *British Medical Journal*, 25 February, **310**: 501–2.

Esping-Anderson, G. (1990) *The Three Worlds of Welfare Capitalism* (Cambridge: Polity Press).

Farnham, D. and Horton, S. (1992) *Managing the New Public Services* (London: Macmillan).

Farnham, D. and Horton, S. (1996) *Managing the New Public Services*, 2nd Edition (London: Macmillan).

Feinberg, J. (1980) *Rights, Justice and the Bounds of Liberty* (Princeton: Princeton University Press).

Femia, J. V. (1985) *Gramsci's Political Thought: Hegemony, Consciousness and the Revolutionary Process* (Oxford: Oxford University Press).

Ferguson, R., Luciano, C. and Vaughan, M. (1991) *Neo-fascism in Europe* (Harlow: Longman).

Fishkin, J. S. (1983) *Justice, Equal Opportunity and the Family* (London: Yale University Press).

Florig, D. (1986) 'The concept of equal opportunity in the analysis of social welfare policy', *Polity*, **XVIII**(3): 392–407.

Foot, P. and Evans, P. (1977) *Why You Should Be A Socialist: The Case for a New Socialist Party* (London: Socialist Workers' Party).

Foot, P. and Evans, P. (1982) *Three Letters to a Bennite from Paul Foot* (London: Socialist Workers' Party).

Forbes, D. (1975) *Hume's Philosophical Politics* (Cambridge: Cambridge University Press).

Forrest, R. and Murie, A. (1984) *Monitoring the Right to Buy* (Bristol: University of Bristol, School of Advanced Urban Studies).

Forrest, R. and Murie, A. (1988) *Selling the Welfare State: The Privatisation of Public Housing* (London: Routledge).

Fortune (2000) *Fortune Global Five Hundred: The World's Largest Companies*, (New York: Time Inc). [http://www.fortune.com/fortune/]

Frankel, C. (1971) 'Equality of Opportunity', *Ethics*, **81**: 191–207.

Frankel, C. (1983) 'Equality of Opportunity' in Letwin, W. (ed.) *Against Equality* (London: Macmillan).

Fraser, D. (1984) *The Evolution of the British Welfare State* (London: Macmillan).

Fraser, N. (1989) *Unruly Practices: Power, Discourse and Gender in Contemporary Social Theory* (Cambridge: Polity Press).

Frazer, E. and Lacey, N. (1993) *The Politics of Community* (London: Harvester Wheatsheaf).

Freeden, M. (1991) *Rights* (Milton Keynes: Open University Press).

Freeman, S. (1999) *John Rawls: Collected Papers* (Cambridge, Mass: Harvard University Press).

Freire, P. (1972) *Pedagogy of the Oppressed* (Harmondsworth: Penguin).

Friedman, M. and Friedman, R. (1980) *Free to Choose* (New York: Harcourt Brace Jovanovich).

Friend, J., Power, J. and Yewlett, C. (1974) *Public Planning: The Intercorporate Dimension* (London: Tavistock).

Fry, E. (1987) *Disabled People and the 1987 General Election* (London: Spastics Society).

Galston, W. (1991) 'Civic Education in the Liberal State' in Rosenblum, N. L. (ed.) *Liberalism and the Moral Life* (Cambridge, Mass: Harvard University Press).

Gaventa, J. (1980) *Power and Powerlessness, Quiescence and Rebellion in an Appalachian Valley* (Oxford: Clarendon Press).

Gazdar, C. (1997) 'Service is "dreadful"', *Community Care*, 26 June: 7.

George, M. (1996) 'From cradle to grave: the future of social care', *Community Care*, 1 August: i–viii.

George, V. (1988) *Wealth, Poverty and Starvation* (Hemel Hempstead: Harvester Wheatsheaf).

George, V. and Manning, N. (1980) *Socialism, Social Welfare and the Soviet Union* (London: Routledge & Kegan Paul).

George, V. and Wilding, P. (1984) *The Impact of Social Policy* (London: Routledge & Kegan Paul).

George, V. and Wilding, P. (1985) *Ideology and Social Welfare* (London: Routledge & Kegan Paul).

Giddens, A. (1984) *The Constitution of Society: Outline of a Theory of Structuration* (Cambridge: Polity Press).

Giddens, A. (1989) *Sociology* (Cambridge: Polity Press).

Giddens, A. (1993) 'Problems of Action and Structure' in Cassell, P. (ed.) *The Giddens Reader* (London: Macmillan).

Giddens, A. (1995) *Politics, Sociology and Social Theory* (Cambridge: Polity Press).

Giddens, A. (1998) *The Third Way: The Renewal of Social Democracy* (Malden, Mass: Polity Press).

Giddens, A. (1999) *Runaway World: The Reith Lectures, 1999* (London: British Broadcasting Coporation).

Gifford, T, (1986) *Independent Inquiry into Disturbances of October 1985 at the Broadwater Farm Estate, Tottenham* (London: Karia Press).

Glendinning, C. (1991) 'Losing ground: social policy and disabled people in Great Britain 1980–1990', *Disability, Handicap and Society*, **6**: 3–19.

Glendinning, C. and Miller, J. (1987) *Women and Poverty* (London: Harvester Wheatsheaf).

Glennerster, H., Power, A. and Travers, T. (1991) 'A new era for social policy: a new enlightenment or a new leviathan?', *Journal of Social Policy*, **20**(3): 389–414.

Goffman, E. (1964) *Stigma, Notes on the Management of Spoiled Identity* (New Jersey: Prentice Hall).

Golding P. (1990) 'Forward' in Lister, R. *The Exclusive Society: Citizenship and the Poor* (London: Child Poverty Action Group).

Gould, C. C. (1988) *Rethinking Democracy: Freedom and Social Cooperation in Politics, Economy and Society* (Cambridge: Cambridge University Press).

Government Statistical Service (1994) *Social Trends* (London: HMSO).

Government Statistical Service (1999) *Health and Personal Social Services Statistics England, 1998 edition* (London: The Stationery Office).

Gqubule, T. (1992) 'Inside Our Chaotic Schools' in Lodge, T. and Nasson, B. (eds) *All, Here, and Now: Black Politics in South Africa in the 1980s* (London: Hurst).

Graham, A. C. (1961) *The Problem of Value* (London: Hutchinson University Library).

Gramsci, A. (1971) *Selections from the Prison Notebooks* [*1948–51*], Hoare, Q. and Smith, G. N. (eds) (London: Lawrence & Wishart).

Grant, L. and Martin, I. (1982) *Immigration Law and Practice* (London: Cobden Trust).

Grant, W. (1992) *Economic Globalisation, Stateless Firms and International Governance* (Coventry: University of Warwick: Department of Politics and International Studies) [Working paper; no. 105].

Gray, T. (1991) *Freedom* (London: Macmillan).

Green, D. (1990) *Equalizing People* (London: Institute of Economic Affairs).

Gregor, A. J. (1997) *Interpretations of Fascism* (New Brunswick: Transaction).

Greve, J. (1991) *Homelessness in Britain* (York: Joseph Rowntree Foundation).

Greve, J., Page, D. and Greve, S. (1971) *Homelessness in London* (Edinburgh: Scottish Academic Press).

Grice, A. (1999) 'CSA reform to simplify payments', *The Independent*, 2 July: 9.

Griffin, J. (1996) *Value Judgement: Improving our Ethical Beliefs* (Oxford: Clarendon Press).

Guba, E. G. and Lincoln, Y. S. (1987) 'The Countenances of Fourth Generation Evaluation: Description, Judgement and Negotiation' in Palumbo, D. J. (ed.) *The Politics of Program Evaluation* (Newbury Park: Sage).

Gunsteren, H. R. (1998) A *Theory of Citizenship: Organizing Plurality in Contemporary Democracies* (Oxford: Westview Press).

Gutch, R. (1989) *The Contract Culture: The Challenge for Voluntary Organisations* (London: National Council for Voluntary Organisations).

Habermas, J. (1981) 'New social movements', *Telos*, **49**, 33–7.

Hall, J. A. and Ikenberry, G. J. (1989) *The State* (Milton Keynes: Open University Press).

Hall, S. (1989) 'The Meaning of New Times' in Hall, S. and Jacques, M. (eds) *New Times* (London: Lawrence & Wishart).

Hallett, C. (1996) *Women and Social Policy, An Introduction* (Hemel Hempstead: Prentice Hall/Harvester Wheatsheaf).

Halsey, A. H. (1988) *British Social Trends since 1900* (London: Macmillan).

Ham, C. and Hill, M. (1984) *The Policy Process in the Modern Capitalist State* (Brighton: Harvester Wheatsheaf).

Harris, D. (1987) *Justifying State Welfare* (Oxford: Basil Blackwell).

Harris, J., Wallace, T. and Booth, H. (1983) *To Ride the Storm: The 1980 Bristol "Riot" and the State* (London: Heinemann Educational).

Harris, R. (1980) *The End of Government ...?* (London: Institute of Economic Affairs).

Harris, R. (1987) *Welfare Without the State: A Quarter-century of Suppressed Public Choice* (London: Institute of Economic Affairs).

Harris, R. (1988) *Beyond the Welfare State: An Economic, Political and Moral Critique of Indiscriminate State Welfare, and a Review of Alternatives to Dependency* (London: Institute of Economic Affairs).

Hayek, F. A. (1960) *The Constitution of Liberty* (London: Routledge & Kegan Paul).

Hawkes, N. and Nuttall, N. (1999) 'Public hostility "hampers UK in science race"', *The Times*, 13 September: 12.

Healey, D. (1989) *The Time of My Life* (London: Penguin).

Heclo, H. (1972) 'Review article: policy analysis', *British Journal of Political Science*, **2**: 83–108.

Higgins, A. (1996a) 'Hong Kong rushes for last way out', *The Guardian*, 1 April: 1.

Higgins, A. (1996b) 'China demands Hong Kong loyalty test', *The Guardian*, 28 March: 15.

Hill, M. (1993) *Understanding Social Policy* (Oxford: Basil Blackwell).

Hill, M. (1996) *Social Policy, A Comparative Analysis* (London: Prentice Hall).

Hill, M. (1997a) *The Policy Process in the Modern State* (London: Prentice Hall/Harvester Wheatsheaf).

Hill, M. (1997b) *The Policy Process: A Reader* (London: Prentice Hall/Harvester Wheatsheaf).

Hill, M. (1998) 'Social Policy and the Political Process' in Alcock, P., Erskine, A. and May, M. *The Student's Companion to Social Policy* (Oxford: Basil Blackwell).

Hill, M. and Bramley, G. (1986) *Analysing Social Policy* (Oxford: Basil Blackwell).

Himmelweit, S. (1988) 'More than a woman's right to choose?' *Feminist Review* (Spring), **29**: 38–56.

Hindess, B. (1993) 'Citizenship in the Modern West' in Turner, B. S. (ed.) *Citizenship and Social Theory* (London: Sage).

Hirst, M. (1987) 'Careers of young people with disabilities between the ages of 16 and 21', *Disability, Handicap and Society*, **2**: 61–75.

Hogwood, B. and Gunn, L. (1984) *Policy Analysis for the Real World* (Oxford: Oxford University Press).

Hohfeld, W. (1919) *Fundamental Legal Conceptions as Applied in Judicial Reasoning* (New Haven: Yale University Press).

Hollingdale, R. J. (1999) *Nietzsche: The Man and His Philosophy* (New York: Cambridge University Press).

Home Office (1999) *The Stephen Lawrence Inquiry: Report of an Inquiry by Sir William Macpherson of Cluny advised by Tom Cook, The Right Reverend Dr John Sentamu, Dr Richard Stone*, Cm 4262-I (London: The Stationery Office).

Hornblower, S. and Spawforth, A. (1998) *The Oxford Companion to Classical Civilization* (Oxford: Oxford University Press).

Howells, J. (1974) *Remember Maria* (London: Butterworths).

Hughes, G. (1996) 'Communitarianism and law and order', *Critical Social Policy*, **49**: 17–41.

Hulley, T. and Clarke, J. (1991) 'Social Problems: Social Construction and Social Causation' in Loney, M. Bocock, R. Clarke, J. *et al.* (eds) *The State or the Market: Politics and Welfare in Contemporary Britain* (London: Sage).

Hyde, M. (1996) 'Fifty years of failure: employment services for disabled people in the UK, *Work, Employment and Society*, **12**(4): 683–700.

Imrie, R. (1996) *Disability and the City: International Perspectives* (London: Paul Chapman Publishing).

Imrie, R. and Wells, P. (1993) 'Disablism, planning and the built environment', *Environment and Planning C: Government and Policy*, **11**(2): 213–31.

Institute for Fiscal Studies (1994) *For Richer, For Poorer: The Changing Distribution of Income in the UK, 1961–1991* (London: Institute for Fiscal Studies).

Jaeger, M. (1943) *Liberty versus Equality* (London: Nelson & Sons).

Jenkins, Robin, (1970) *Exploitation: The World Power Structure and the Inequality of Nations* (London: MacGibbon & Kee).

Jenkins, W. (1978) *Policy Analysis: A Political and Organisational Perspective* (London: Martin Robertson).

Jones, P. (1994) *Rights* (London: Macmillan).

Jordan, B. (1998) *New Politics of Welfare: Social Justice in a Global Context* (London: Sage).

Joseph, K. and Sumption, J. (1979) *Equality* (London: John Murray).

Kallianes, V. and Rubenfeld, P. (1997) 'Disabled women and reproductive rights', *Disability and Society*, **12**(2): 203–21.

Kandola, B. (1993) 'Managing diversity', *Viewpoint: The Magazine for Benefits Agency Managers* (Summer), **8**: 18.

Kandola, R. and Fullerton, J. (1984) *Managing the Mosaic, Diversity in Action* (London: Institute of Personnel Management).

Kandola, R., Fullerton, J. and Ahmed, Y. (1995) 'Managing diversity: Succeeding where equal opportunities has failed', *Equal Opportunities Review*, Jan/Feb, **59**: 31–6.

Kant, I. (1786) *Critique of Pure Reason* [1998 edition: P. Guyer and A. W. Wood (eds)] (Cambridge: Cambridge University Press).

Karol, K. S. (1967) *China: The Other Communism* (London: Heinemann).

Kedward, H. R. (1969) *Fascism in Western Europe 1900–45* (London: Blackie & Son).

Kiely, R. and Marfleet, P. (eds) (1998) *Globalisation and the Third World* (London: Routledge).

Kriesi, H., Koopmans R., Dyvendak, J. W. and Giugni, M. G. (1995) *New Social Movements in Western Europe: A Comparative Analysis* (London: UCL Press).

Kropotkin, P. (1987) *Anarchism and Anarchist Communism* (London: Freedom Press).

Kukathas, C. and Pettit, P. (1990) *Rawls: A Theory of Justice and its Critics* (Cambridge: Polity Press).

Kunz, C., Jones, R. and Spencer, K. (1989) *Bidding for Change?* (Birmingham: Birmingham Settlement).

Kymlicka, W. (1989) *Liberalism, Community and Culture* (Oxford: Clarendon Press).

Kymlicka, W. (1990) Contemporary *Political Philosophy: An Introduction* (Oxford: Clarendon Press).

Kymlicka, W. and Norman, W. (2000) *Citizenship in Diverse Societies* (New York: Oxford University Press).

Labour Party (1994) *Jobs and Social Justice* (London: Labour Party).

Landale, J. and Bowditch, G. (1997) 'Blair salutes his female army' *The Times*, 8 May: 10.

Langan, M. and Clarke, J. (1994) 'Managing in the Mixed Economy of Care' in Clarke, J., Cochrane, A. and McLaughlin, E. (eds) *Managing Social Policy*, (London: Sage).

Langhorne, J. and Langhorne, W. (eds) (1858) *Plutarch's Lives* (London: William Tegg).

Laqueur, W. (1991) *Fascism: A Reader's Guide* (Aldershot: Scolar Press).

Laski, H. (1969) 'Liberty and Equality' in Blackstone, W. T. (ed.) *The Concept of Equality* (Minneapolis: Burgess).

Laver, M. (1979) *The Politics of Private Desires* (Harmondsworth: Penguin).

Lawrence, A. (1998) *China under Communism* (London: Routledge).

Lebacqz, K. (1986) *Six Theories of Justice* (Minneapolis: Augsburg).

Ledger, S. and McCracken, S. (1995) *Cultural Politics at the Fin de Siècle* (Cambridge: Cambridge University Press).

Lee, P. and Raban, C. (1988) *Welfare Theory and Social Policy: Reform or Revolution?* (London: Sage).

Le Grand, J., Propper, C. and Robinson, R. (1992) *The Economics of Social Problems*, 3rd Edition (London: Macmillan).

Lehning, P. B. and Weale, A. (eds) (1997) *Citizenship, Democracy, and Justice in the New Europe* (London: Routledge).

Leigh-Doyle, S. (1996) *Social Exclusion: A Major Challenge for Public Welfare Services* (Luxembourg: OOPEC).

Lemert, E. (1962) *Human Deviance, Social Problems and Social Control* (New Jersey: Prentice Hall).

Lemon, A. (1976) *Apartheid: A Geography of Separation* (Farnborough: Saxon House).

Letwin, W. (ed) (1983) *Against Equality: Readings on Economic and Social Policy* (London: Macmillan).

Levin, P. (1997) *Making Social Policy* (Buckingham: Open University Press).

Levitas, R. (1998) *The Inclusive Society? Social Exclusion and New Labour* (London: Macmillan).

Lifton, R. J. (1986) *The Nazi Doctors: Medical Killings and the Psychology of Genocide* (Basingstoke: Macmillan).

Lindblom, C. (1959) 'The science of "muddling through" ', *Public Administration Review*, **19**: 78–88.

Lindblom, C. (1977) *Politics and Markets* (New York: Basic Books).

Lipset, S. (1969) *Revolution and Counterrevolution: Change and Persistence in Social Structures* (London: Heinemann Educational).

Lister, R. (1990) *The Exclusive Society, Citizenship and the Poor* (London: Child Poverty Action Group).

Lister, R. (1997) *Citizenship: Feminist Perspectives* (London: Macmillan).

Loney, M., Bocock, R., Clarke, J. *et al.* (1991) *The State or the Market: Politics and Welfare in Contemporary Britain* (London: Sage).

Long, D. (1977) *Bentham on Liberty* (Toronto: University of Toronto Press).

Lonsdale, S. (1986) *Work and Inequality* (Harlow: Longman).

Lonsdale, S. (1990) *Women and Disability: The Experience of Physical Disability among Women* (London: Macmillan).

Lowe, R. (1993) *The Welfare State in Britain since 1945* (London: Macmillan).

Lukes, S. (1974) *Power: A Radical View* (London: Macmillan).

Lukes, S. (1991) 'Equality and Liberty, in Held D. (ed.) *Political Theory Today* (Cambridge: Polity Press).

Lund, B. (1996) *Housing Problems and Housing Policy* (London: Longman).

Macaskill, E. (1996) 'Tory civil war: Euro-sceptics plot revenge', *The Guardian*, 9 December: 15.

MacCallum, G. C. (1967) 'Negative and positive freedom' *Philosophical Review*, **76**: 312–34.

McCarthy, M. (1989) *The New Politics of Welfare: An Agenda for the 1990s* (London: Macmillan).

McCloskey, H. J. (1966) 'Egalitarianism, equality and justice', *Australasian Journal of Philosophy*, May: 50–69.

McCrudden, C. (1998) 'The Equality of Opportunity Duty in the Northern Ireland Act 1998: An Analysis', *Equality and Human Rights: Their Role in Peace Building* (Belfast: Committee on the Administration of Justice).

MacDonald, R. (1997) *Youth, the 'Underclass' and Social Exclusion* (London: Routledge).

MacIntyre, A. (1981) *After Virtue* (London: Duckworth).

MacIntyre, A. (1988) *Whose Justice? Which Rationality?* (London: Duckworth).

MacIntyre, A. (1996) *Whose Justice? Which Rationality?*, 2nd Edition (London: Duckworth).

MacKinnon, A. and Gatens, M. (1998) *Gender and Institutions: Welfare, Work & Citizenship* (Cambridge: Cambridge University Press).

Mackintosh, J. (1968) *The Devolution of Power: Local Democracy, Regionalism and Nationalism* (Harmondsworth: Penguin).

McLennan, G. (1989) *Marxism, Pluralism and Beyond* (Cambridge: Polity Press).

Macmillan, H. (1938) *The Middle Way* (London: Macmillan & Co.).

Macmillan, H. (1978) *The Middle Way: A Study of the Problem of Economic and Social Progress in a Free and Democratic Society* (Wakefield: EP Publishing).

Major, J. (1997) *Our Nation's Future: Keynote Speeches on the Principles and Convictions that Shape Conservative Policies* (London: Conservative Political Centre).

Major, J. (1999) *John Major: The Autobiography* (London: HarperCollins).

Malpass, P. and Murie, A. (1994) *Housing Policy and Practice* (London: Mac-millan).

Mandelson, P. (1997) *Labour's Next Steps: Tackling Social Exclusion* (London: Fabian Pamphlet No. 581).

Mann, K. (1994) 'Watching the defectives: Observers of the underclass in the USA, Britain and Australia', *Critical Social Policy*, **41**: 79–99.

Marquand, D. (1997) *The New Reckoning: Capitalism, States and Citizens* (Cambridge: Polity Press).

Marshall, T. H. (1950) *Citizenship and Social Class, and Other Essays* (Cambridge: Cambridge University Press).

Marshall, T. H. (1992) *Citizenship and Social Class* (London: Pluto Press).

Marshall, G., Swift, A. and Roberts, S. (1996) *Against the Odds? Social Justice in Modern Britain* (Oxford: Clarendon Press).

Martin, J. and White, A. (1988) *Surveys of Disabled People in Great Britain: Report No. 2, The Financial Circumstances of Disabled Adults Living in Private Households* (London: OPCS).

Martin, J., White, A. and Meltzer, H. (1989) *Disabled Adults: Services, Transport and Employment* (London: OPCS).

Marx, K. (1938) *Critique of the Gotha Programme* (London: Lawrence & Wishart).

Maslow, A. H. (1943) *A Theory of Human Motivation* (Indianapolis, Ind: Bobbs-Merrill).

Maslow, A. H. (1968) *Toward a Psychology of Being* (New York: Van Nostrand Reinhold).

Mathey, K. (1990) *Housing Policies in the Socialist Third World* (London: Mansell).

Mead, L. M. (1986) *Beyond Entitlement: The Social Obligations of Citizenship* (New York: Free Press).

Meli, F. (1988) *A History of the ANC: South Africa Belongs to Us* (London: James Currey).

Melucci, A. (1989) *Nomads of the Present: Social Movements and Individual Needs in Contemporary Society* (London: Hutchinson Radius).

Mendus, S. (1989) *Toleration and the Limits of Liberalism* (London: Macmillan).

Meredith, M. (1988) *In the Name of Apartheid: South Africa in the Postwar Period* (London: Hamilton).

Michaelman, F. I. (1989) 'Constitutional Welfare Rights and "A Theory of Justice"' in Daniels, N. (ed.) *Reading Rawls: Critical Studies on Rawls's A Theory of Justice* (Stanford: Stanford University Press).

Middlemas, K. (1979) *Politics in Industrial Society* (London: André Deutsch).

Midgley, J. (1997) Social *Welfare in Global Context* (London: Sage).

Mihill, C. (1996) '£160,000 cost for care of dying girl "worth it"', *The Guardian*, July, 19: 9.

Miles, R. (1988) *Racism* (London: Routledge).

Miliband, R. (1969a) *The State in Capitalist Society* (London: Weidenfeld & Nicolson).

Miliband, R. (1969b) ' The capitalist state: Reply to Nicos Poulantzas', *New Left Review*, **59**: 53–60.

Mill, J. S. (1859) *On Liberty* (London: Parker).

Miller, D. (1995) Introduction in Miller, D. and Walzer, M. *Pluralism, Justice and Equality* (Oxford: Oxford University Press).

Miller, D. and Walzer, M. (1995) *Pluralism, Justice and Equality* (Oxford: Oxford University Press).

Miller, T. C. (ed.) (1984) *Public Sector Performance: A Conceptual Turning Point* (Baltimore: John Hopkins Press).

Milne, A. J. M. (1968) *Freedom and Rights* (London: George Allen & Unwin).

Minford, P. (1991) 'The Role of the Social Services: A View from the New Right' in Loney, M., Bocock, R., Clarke, J. *et al.* (eds) *The State or the Market: Politics and Welfare in Contemporary Britain* (London: Sage).

Minford, P., Peel, M. and Ashton, P. (1987) *The Housing Morass*, Hobart Papers 25, (London: Institute of Economic Affairs).

Mingione, E. (ed.) (1996) *Urban Poverty and the Underclass: A Reader* (Oxford: Basil Blackwell).

Mishra, R. (1981) *Society and Social Policy: Theories and Practice of Welfare* (London: Macmillan).

Moore, G. E. (1959) *Principia Ethica* (Cambridge: Cambridge University Press).

Moorehead, C. (1989) *Betrayal: Child Exploitation in Today's World* (London: Barrie & Jenkins).

Morris, L. (1994) *Dangerous Classes: The Underclass and Social Citizenship* (London: Routledge).

Mount, F. (1986) *The Practice of Liberty* (London: Conservative Political Centre).

Mouzelis, N. (1975) *Organisation and Bureaucracy: An Analysis of Modern Theories* (London: Routledge & Kegan Paul).

Mukerjee, R. (1964) *The Dimensions of Values* (London: George Allen & Unwin).

Mulhall, S. and Swift, A. (1992) *Liberals and Communitarians* (Oxford: Basil Blackwell).

Murray, C. (1990) *The Emerging British Underclass* (London: Institute of Economic Affairs).

Murray, C. (1994) *Underclass: The Crisis deepens* [commentaries by P. Alcock, *et al.*]. (London: Institute of Economic Affairs Health and Welfare Unit).

Murray, C. A. (1996) *The Underclass: The Developing Debate* [commentaries R. Lister, ed.] (London: Institute of Economic Affairs Health and Welfare Unit and *The Sunday Times*).

National Council for Civil Liberties (1951) *50,000 Outside the Law* (London: National Council for Civil Liberties).

Newman, J. and Clarke, J. (1994) 'Going About Our Business? The managerialization of public services, in Clarke, J., Cochrane, A. and McLaughlin, E. (eds) *Managing Social Policy* (London: Sage).

Newton, M., Hall, S. and Crick, B. (1992) *Is Equality Dead?* (London: Fabian Society).

NHS Executive (1998) *Quarterly Review*, October–December, 1998.

Nisse, J. (1998) 'Harmon poised for change at Benefits Agency', *The Times*, 14 May: 28.

Norman, R. (1987) *Free and Equal: A Philosophical Examination of Political Values* (Oxford: Oxford University Press).

Novak, T. (1988) *Poverty and the State* (Milton Keynes: Open University Press).

Nozick, R. (1974) *Anarchy, State and Utopia* (Oxford: Basil Blackwell).

Nuttall, N. (1999) 'Europe moves against GM food research', *The Times*, 6 September: 2.

Oakeshott, M. (1975) *On Human Conduct* (Oxford: Oxford University Press).

Office for National Statistics (1998a) *Annual Abstract of Statistics, 1998 edition* (London: Office for National Statistics).

Office for National Statistics (1998b) *Regional Trends, 1998 edition*, vol. 33 (London: Office for National Statistics).

Office for National Statistics (2000) *Social Trends, 2000 edition*, vol. 30 (London: Government Statistical Service).

Office of Population Censuses and Surveys (1993) *The 1991 Census: Report for Great Britain* (*Part One*) (London: HMSO).

Olds, K. (ed.) (1999) *Globalisation and the Asia Pacific: Contested Territories*, (London: Routledge).

Oliver, M. (1990) *The Politics of Disablement* (London: Macmillan).

Oliver, M. (1996) *Understanding Disability: From Theory to Practice* (London: Macmillan).

Oliver, M. and Barnes, C. (1998) *Disabled People and Social Policy* (Harlow: Addison Wesley Longman).

O'Neilly, J. (1995) 'When prejudice is not just skin deep', *People Management*, 23 February: 34–7.

Oommen, T. K. (1997) *Citizenship and National Identity: From Colonialism to Globalism* (London: Sage).

O'Sullivan, N. (1983) *Modern Ideologies: Fascism* (London: J. M. Dent & Sons).

Owen, D. (1991) *Time to Declare* (London: Penguin).

Owen, D. (1995) *Nietzsche: Politics and Modernity: Critique of Liberal Reason* (London: Sage).

Page, E. (1985) *Political Authority and Bureaucratic Power: A Comparative Analysis* (Brighton: Wheatsheaf).

Pagel, N. (1988) *On Our Own Behalf* (Manchester: Greater Manchester Coalition of Disabled People).

Pahl, J. (1989) *Money and Marriage* (London: Macmillan).

Panikkar, K. N. (1995) 'Culture and globalisation' *Economic and Political Weekly*, **30**: 374–5.

Parekh, B. (1992) 'A Case for Positive Discrimination' in Hepple, B. and Szyszczak, E. M. (eds) *Discrimination: The Limits of Law* (London: Mansell).

Parsons, T. (1966) *Societies: Evolutionary and Comparative Perspectives* (Englewood Cliffs: Prentice Hall).

Parsons, T. (1971) *The System of Modern Societies* (Englewood Cliffs: Prentice Hall).

Parsons, W. (1995) *Public Policy: An Introduction to the Theory and Practice of Policy Analysis* (Aldershot: Edward Elgar).

Pateman, C. (1988) *The Sexual Contract* (Cambridge: Polity Press).

Pateman, C. (1989) The *Disorder of Women* (Cambridge: Polity Press).

Peach, C., Robinson, V., Maxted, J. and Chance, J. (1988) 'Immigration and Ethnicity' in Halsey, A. H. (ed.) *British Social Trends since 1900* (London: Macmillan).

Pearson, M. (1986) 'The Politics of Ethnic Minority Health Studies' in Rothwell, T. and Phillips, D. (eds) *Health, Race and Ethnicity* (London: Croom Helm).

Phillips, A. (ed.) (1987) *Feminism and Equality* (Oxford: Blackwell).

Phillips, A. (1991) *Engendering Democracy* (Oxford: Polity Press).

Phillips, A. (1992) 'Universal Pretensions in Political Thought' in Barrett, M. and Phillips, A. (eds) *Destabilizing Theory* (Cambridge: Polity Press).

Phillips, A. (ed.) (1998) *Feminism and Politics* (Oxford: Oxford University Press).

Pilkington, E. and Mihill, C. (1996) 'Never give up unless you are just on the last little drop of life you have in you', *The Guardian*, 23 May: 1.

Pithouse, A. and Williamson, H. (1997) *Engaging the User in Welfare Services* (Birmingham: Ventura Press).

Pixley, J. (1993) *Citizenship and Employment: Investigating Post-industrial Options* (New York: Cambridge University Press).

Plant, R. (1984) *Equality, Markets and the State* (London: Fabian Society).

Plant, R. (1988) *Citizenship, Rights and Socialism* (London: Fabian Society).

Plant, R. (1990) *Citizenship and Rights in Thatcher's Britain* (London: Institute of Economic Affairs Health and Welfare Unit).

Plant, R. (1993) *Social Justice, Labour and the New Right* (London: Fabian Society).

Plant, R., Lesser, H. and Taylor-Gooby, P. (1980) *Political Philosophy and Social Welfare: Essays on the Normative Basis of Welfare Provision* (London: Routledge & Kegan Paul).

Popper, K. (1945) *The Open Society and its Enemies* (London: Routledge & Kegan Paul).

Poulantzas, N. (1969) 'The problem of the capitalist state', *New Left Review*, **58**: 67–78.

Priestley, M. (1999) *Disability Politics and Community Care* (London: Jessica Kingsley).

Prior, D., Stewart, J. and Walsh, K. (1995) *Citizenship: Rights, Community and Participation* (London: Pitman Publishing).

Prior, J. (1986) *A Balance of Power* (London: Hamilton).

Quest Financial Services (1999) *School Fees Planning* (Chipping Norton, Oxon: Quest Financial Services). [www.questfs.co.uk/qten.htm]

RADAR (1993) *Disability and Discrimination in Employment* (London: RADAR).

Raison, T. (1990) *Tories and the Welfare State: A History of Conservative Social Policy since the Second World War* (London: Macmillan).

Rawls, J. (1972) *A Theory of Justice* (Cambridge, Mass: Harvard University Press).

Rees, J. (1971) *Equality* (London: Pall Mall Press).

Reid, I. (1986) *The Sociology of School and Education* (London: Fontana).

Reid, I., Williams, R. and Rayner, M. (1991) 'The Education of the Elite' in Walford, G. (ed.) *Private Schooling: Tradition, Change and Diversity*, (London: Paul Chapman Publishing).

Rhodes, T. (1999) 'Bitter harvest: the real story of Monsanto and GM food', *The Times*, 22 August: 1.

Rich, R. F. (ed.) (1979) *Translating Evaluation into Policy* (London: Sage).

Rist, R. (ed.) (1995) *Policy Evaluation: Linking Theory to Practice* (Aldershot: Edward Elgar).

Roche, M. (1992) *Rethinking Citizenship: Welfare, Ideology, and Change in Modern Society* (Cambridge: Polity Press).

Roche, M. and Van Berkel, R. (1997) *European Citizenship and Social Exclusion* (Aldershot: Ashgate).

Rolfe, H. (1999) *Gender Equality and the Careers Service* (Manchester: Equal Opportunities Commission).

Rollinson, D., Broadfield, A. and Edwards, D. (1998) *Organisational Behaviour and Analysis: An Integrated Approach* (Harlow: Addison Wesley Longman).

Rorty, R. (1989) *Contingency, Irony and Solidarity* (Cambridge: Cambridge University Press).

Rossi, P. H. and Williams, W. (1972) *Evaluating Social Programs* (New York: Seminar Press).

Rousseau, J. J. (1762) *The Social Contract* [1968 translation by Maurice Cranston] (Harmondsworth: Penguin).

Rumbaugh, D. M. (1977) *Language Learning by a Chimpanzee: The Lana Project* (New York: Academic Press).

Russell, B. (1949) 'Individual and Social Ethics' in his *Authority and the Individual* (London: George Allen & Unwin).

Sandel, M. (1982) *Liberalism and the Limits of Justice* (Cambridge: Cambridge University Press).

Sanderson, M. (1987) *Educational Opportunity and Social Change in England* (London: Faber & Faber).

Saunders, P. (1993), 'Citizenship in a Liberal Society' in Turner, B. S. (ed.) *Citizenship and Social Theory* (London: Sage).

Savage-Rumbaugh, E. S. (1986) *Ape Language: From Conditioned Response to Symbol* (Oxford: Oxford University Press).

Savage-Rumbaugh, E. S., Shanker, S. and Taylor, T. J. (1998) *Apes, Language, and the Human Mind* (New York: Oxford University Press).

Schnytzer, A. (1982) *Stalinist Economic Strategy in Practice* (Oxford: Oxford University Press).

Schumann, F. (1966) *Ideology and Organization in Communist China* (Berkeley: University of California).

Schwarzmantel, J. (1994) *The State in Contemporary Society* (Hemel Hempstead: Harvester Wheatsheaf).

Scott, R. (1996) *Report of the Inquiry into the Export of Defence Equipment and Dual-use Goods to Iraq and Related Prosecutions* (London: HMSO).

Scruton, R. (1982) *A Dictionary of Political Thought* (London: Macmillan).

Scruton, R. (1984) *The Meaning of Conservatism*, 2nd Edition (London: Macmillan).

Seedat, A. (1984) *Crippling a Nation: Health in Apartheid South Africa* (London: International Defence and Aid Fund for South Africa).

Seidman S. and Wagner, D. (1992) *Postmodernism and Social Theory* (Oxford: Basil Blackwell).

Seldon, A. (1981) *Whither the Welfare State?* (London: Institute of Economic Affairs).

Seldon, A. (1983) *Agenda for Social Democracy: Essays on the Prospects for New Economic Thinking and Policy in the Changing British Political Scene* (London: Institute of Economic Affairs).

Shaw, G. B. (1913) *Case for Equality*, paper delivered at the National Liberal Club, 1 May.

Sillince, J. (1990) *Housing Policies in Eastern Europe and the Soviet Union* (London: Routledge).

Silver, H. (1973) *Equal Opportunity in Education: A Reader in Social Class and Educational Opportunity* (London: Methuen).

Simon, H. A. (1957) *Administrative Behaviour* (New York: Macmillan).

Simon, H. A. (1969) *The Sciences of the Artificial* (Cambridge, Mass: MIT Press).

Sly, F. (1996) 'Disability and the labour market', *Labour Market Trends*, September: 413–24.

Smith, A. (1776) *An Inquiry into the Nature and Causes of the Wealth of Nations* (London: Strahan & Cadell).

Smith, D. J. (1992) *Understanding the Underclass* (London: Policy Studies Institute).

Smith, D. M. (1982) *Living under Apartheid* (London: George Allen & Unwin).

Smith, S. (1996) *The Politics of 'Race' and Residence: Citizenship, Segregation and White Supremacy in Britain* (Cambridge: Polity Press).

Smithers, R. (1996) '2.2 million Hong Kong Chinese to get no-visa access to Britain' *The Guardian*, 4 March: 1.

Socialist Party of Great Britain (1948) *The Communist Manifesto and the Socialist Party of Great Britain* (London: Socialist Party of Great Britain).

Sternhell, Z. (1994) *The Birth of Fascist Ideology: From Cultural Rebellion to Political Revolution* (Princeton: Princeton University Press).

Stefanaq, P. (1981) *A History of Albania from its Origins to the Present Day* (London: Routledge & Kegan Paul).

Stevens, L. (1982) *John Stuart Mill and Liberty: a Re-evaluation* (Sheffield: Sheffield City Polytechnic, Department of Political Studies).

Stoljar, S. (1984) *An Analysis of Rights* (New York: St Martin's Press).

Sullivan, M. (1994) *Modern Social Policy* (Hemel Hempstead: Harvester Wheatsheaf).

Swain, J., Finkelstein, V., French, S. and Oliver, M. (eds) (1993) *Disabling Barriers, Enabling Environments* (London: Sage).

Symonds, A. and Kelly, A. (1998) *The Social Construction of Community Care* (London: Macmillan).

Tapper, T. (1997) *Fee-paying Schools and Educational Change in Britain: Between the State and the Marketplace* (London: Woburn Press).

Tawney, R. H. (1926) *Religion and the Rise of Capitalism* (London: Murray).

Tawney, R. H. (1964) *Equality* (London: George Allen & Unwin).

Taylor, C. (1979) 'What's Wrong with Negative Liberty?' in Ryan, A. *The Idea of Freedom* (Oxford: Oxford University Press).

Taylor, D. (1992) 'The Big Idea for the nineties? The rise of the citizen's charters', *Critical Social Policy*, **33**: 87–94.

Taylor-Parker, S. and Gibson, K. R. (eds) (1990) *'Language' and Intelligence in Monkeys and Apes: Comparative Developmental Perspectives* (New York: Cambridge University Press).

Tebbit, N. (1986) *The Values of Freedom* (London: Conservative Political Centre).

Thane, P. (1982) *The Foundation of the Welfare State* (London: Longman).

Thatcher, M. (1968) *What's Wrong with Politics?* (London: Conservative Political Centre).

Thatcher, M. (1993) *The Downing Street Years* (London: HarperCollins).

Thomson, D. (1949) *Equality* (Cambridge: Cambridge University Press).

Thomson, D. (1969) 'The Problem of Equality' in Blackstone, W. T. (ed.) *The Concept of Equality* (Minneapolis: Burgess).

Thurlow, R. (1999) *Fascism* (Cambridge: Cambridge University Press).

Timmins, N. (1996) *The Five Giants: A Biography of the Welfare State* (London: Fontana).

Titmuss, R. M. (1958) *Essays on the Welfare State* (London: George Allen & Unwin).

Titmuss, R. M. (1974) *Social Policy: An Introduction* (London: George Allen & Unwin).

Titmuss, R. M. (1987) *The Philosophy of Welfare* (London: George Allen & Unwin).

Torrance, J. (1977) *Estrangement, Alienation and Exploitation: A Sociological Approach to Historical Materialism* (London: Macmillan).

Touraine, A. (1977) *The Self-Production of Society* (Chicago: University of Chicago Press).

Touraine, A. (1981) *The Voice and the Eye: An Analysis of Social Movements* (Cambridge: Cambridge University Press).

Townsend, P. (1979) *Poverty in the United Kingdom* (Harmondsworth: Penguin).

Tullock, G. (1997) 'The Economic Theory of Bureaucracy' in Hill, M. (ed.) *The Policy Process: A Reader*, 2nd Edition (London: Prentice Hall).

Turner, B. S. (1986) *Equality* (London: Tavistock).

Turner, B. S. (1993) *Citizenship and Social Theory* (London: Sage).

Twine, F. (1994) *Citizenship and Social Rights: The Interdependence of Self and Society* (London: Sage).

Vincent, A. (1987) *Theories of the State* (Oxford: Basil Blackwell).

Vincent, A. (1992) *Modern Political Ideologies* (Oxford: Basil Blackwell).

Voet, R. (1998) *Feminism and Citizenship* (London: Sage).

Vogler, R. (1991) *Reading the Riot Act: The Magistracy, the Police and the Army in Civil Disorder* (Milton Keynes: Open University Press).

Walford, G. (1990) *Privatization and Privilege in Education* (London: Routledge).

Walker, A. (1980) 'The social creation of poverty and dependency in old age', *Journal of Social Policy*, **9**(1): 49–75.

Walker, A. (1982a) 'The social consequences of early retirement', *Political Quarterly*, **53**(1): 61–72.

Walker, A. (1982b) *Unqualified and Underemployed* (London: Macmillan).

Walker, A. (1986) 'Pensions and the Production of Poverty in Old Age' in Phillipson, C. and Walker, A. (eds) *Ageing and Social Policy* (Aldershot: Gower).

Walker, B. (1981) *Welfare Economics and Urban Problems* (London: Hutchinson).

Walker, D. (1982) 'Norwich loses appeal on sale of houses', *The Times*, 10 February: 4.

Walker, P. (1991) *Staying Power* (London: Bloomsbury).

Walker, R. L. (1991) *Thinking about Workfare: Evidence from the USA* (London: HMSO).

Walters, A. (1986) *Britain's Economic Renaissance: Margaret Thatcher's Reforms, 1979–1984* (Oxford: Oxford University Press).

Walzer, M. (1970) *Obligations: Essays on Disobedience, War, and Citizenship* (London: Oxford University Press).

Walzer, M. (1983) *Spheres of Justice: A Defence of Pluralism and Equality* (Oxford: Robertson).

Waters, M. (1994) *Modern Sociological Theory* (London: Sage).

Weiss, C. H. (1972) *Evaluation Research: Methods of Assessing Program Effectiveness* (Englewood Cliffs: Prentice Hall).

White, A. (1984) *Rights* (Oxford: Clarendon Press).

White, D. (1972) 'The problem of power', *British Journal of Political Sciences*, **2**: 479–90.

White, M. (1997) 'At war with his party' *The Guardian*, 17 April: 1.

Wilcox, S. (1995) *Housing Finance Review, 1995/6* (York: Joseph Rowntree Foundation).

Williams, F. (1989) *Social Policy: A Critical Introduction* (Cambridge: Polity Press).

Williams, F. (1992) 'Somewhere Over the Rainbow', in Manning, N. and Page, R. (eds) *Social Policy Review 4* (London: Longman).

Winkler, J. (1977) 'The Corporate Economy, Theory and Administration' in Scase, R. (ed.) *Industrial Society: Class, Cleavage and Control* (London: George Allen & Unwin).

Winkler, F. (1987) 'Consumerism in health care: Beyond the supermarket model' *Policy and Politics*, **15**(1): 1–8.

Winnifrith, T. (1992) *Perspectives on Albania* (London: Macmillan).

Wistow, G., Knapp, M., Hardy, B. and Allen, C. (1994) *Social Care in a Mixed Economy* (Buckingham: Open University Press).

Wolf, M. (1992) *A Thrice-Told Tale: Feminism, Postmodernism, and Ethnographic Responsibility* (California: Stanford University Press).

Wolff, J. (1991) *Robert Nozick: Property, Justice and the Minimal State* (Cambridge: Polity Press).

Wolff, R. (1977) *Understanding Rawls: A Reconstruction and Critique of 'A Theory of Justice'* (Princeton: Princeton University Press).

World Bank (2000) *World Development Data: Total GDP, 1998, Rank Order* (World Bank). [http://www.worldbank.org/data/databytopic/keyrefs.html]

Young, H. (1995) 'No passport from Hong Kong', *The Guardian*, 26 September: 15.

Young, H. (1996) 'Fighting in the water as the boat sinks', *The Guardian*, 10 December: 15.

Young, I. M. (1990) *Justice and the Politics of Difference* (Princeton: Princeton University Press).

Index

Note: references to figures and tables are indicated by italics (e.g. 64*f*, 34*t*).